KNOW

GROW

EXIT

HOW ENTREPRENEURS GROW AND FINISH FAST

KNOW GROW EXIT

W. CLIFF OXFORD

ForbesBooks

Published by ForbesBooks, Charleston, South Carolina.
Member of Advantage Media Group.

ForbesBooks is a registered trademark, and the ForbesBooks colophon is a trademark of Forbes Media, LLC.

Printed in the United States of America.

10 9 8 7 6 5 4 3 2 1

ISBN: 978-1-950863-09-9
LCCN: 2019941930

Book design by Jamie Wise

This publication is designed to provide accurate and authoritative information in regard to the subject matter covered. It is sold with the understanding that the publisher is not engaged in rendering legal, accounting, or other professional services. If legal advice or other expert assistance is required, the services of a competent professional person should be sought.

Advantage Media Group is proud to be a part of the Tree Neutral® program. Tree Neutral offsets the number of trees consumed in the production and printing of this book by taking proactive steps such as planting trees in direct proportion to the number of trees used to print books. To learn more about Tree Neutral, please visit www.treeneutral.com.

Since 1917, the Forbes mission has remained constant. Global Champions of Entrepreneurial Capitalism. ForbesBooks exists to further that aim by bringing the Stories, Passion, and Knowledge of top thought leaders to the forefront. ForbesBooks brings you The Best in Business. To be considered for publication, please visit www.forbesbooks.com.

I dedicate this book to my daughter, Emily, who lives her life every day to help the most people she can and my son, Nick, who lives to see a bright spot ahead.

VISIT US ONLINE TO ACCESS THESE FREE RESOURCES

WHAT YOU NEED TO KNOW ONE MINUTE BEFORE DAYLIGHT

The Morning Report™ is one of the most highly anticipated daily emails for CEO entrepreneurs around the globe. In less than 2 minutes, the Morning Report provides a summary of all the essential news items that matter to people who own and run businesses.

→ SUBSCRIBE AT GETTHEMORNINGREPORT.COM

IS YOUR BUSINESS ATTRACTIVE TO A BUYER?

Thinking of selling your business? Does your company have the 7 Elements of a Valuable Business? Our 7E Assessment will uncover your core strengths, areas of weakness, and hidden assets so you can maximize the value of your most valuable asset.

→ TAKE THE 7E ASSESSMENT AT OXFORDCENTER.COM/7E
Your score will be emailed to you within seconds of submitting

APPLY TO BE AN OXFORD CENTER MEMBER

Oxford Center for Entrepreneurs is an exclusive membership community that brings together second-stage and high-growth CEO entrepreneurs interested in accelerating their growth through education, shared insights, and commerce connections that push their thinking and businesses forward. We support our members with our no-nonsense Know-Grow-Exit education and Entrepreneur Briefings that feature leading CEOs that have grown multimillion- and billion-dollar companies.

→ APPLY FOR MEMBERSHIP AT OXFORDCENTER.COM/APPLY

TABLE OF CONTENTS

STAY IN YOUR LANE, BRO

Entrepreneurs love to learn, but they also want information that's concise and straight to the point. I insisted on writing a prelude to this book because as an entrepreneur, it's easy to get distracted by shiny objects. But avoiding those and staying focused on your niche is the only way to survive through fast growth. That's what it's all about when you're growing a company and finishing fast—surviving. Survive and then some luck comes your way. That's how most companies are built.

I saw this book in a nutshell in the wake of the 2019 Super Bowl, where everyone was complaining about boredom and bad commercials. My answer: Was there anything we could learn from it? Yes. Don't make bad decisions and bad bets like I did against New England. It was not rational. Entrepreneurs should step back when they see the following circumstances:

First, I was emotional. I wanted Brady to lose because I was still carrying around grievances about the 2017 Super Bowl, when the Falcons blew a huge lead to him. You've got to let losses go if they are not impacting your life or business.

Next, I had been on a hot streak and thought I'd gotten smart. All bets should be judged independently, and you should never make a "let it ride" decision right after one or two big wins, or right after somebody tells you that you have the Midas touch. My magic vanished with the hard work of New England's coaching staff to confuse the young Rams quarterback. I would have seen that coming if I had not been counting my money at the table thinking I was going to win.

Stay in your lane, bro. I'm a lot more qualified to be betting against Papa John's comeback than I am to be betting on who is going to win a Super Bowl. The fact is, we enjoy getting out of our lane—chasing shiny objects. We can't help ourselves. It is the most recurring mistake I see in entrepreneurship every day, and here I am thinking I'm a pro football expert.

I know this was just a bad bet on football, but when I've made bad bets in business, the failures could be traced to either emotion or lack of focus, and the biggest falls were when I've gotten too smart overnight from a win.

What do you do after the fall? Live, learn, and try to find a positive so your feet can hit the floor running the next day. By the way, Gladys Knight was worth the price of admission and yes, Brady is the greatest of all time.

WELCOME TO THE SWAMP— THE TREACHEROUS PATH TO GROWING AND EXITING YOUR BUSINESS

The phrase "I am up to my ass in alligators" describes the most common human condition among entrepreneurs. It was perfect for me—because when I was twelve, I decided to paddle from Gator Creek to the Atlantic with my brother, Kenny, and my cousin Walter.

What we set off on would turn out to be more than a lazy cruise. Between that launch in Ware County, Georgia, and the Atlantic was the Okefenokee Swamp—a seven-hundred-square-mile bog that dates back to the dinosaurs. I grew up on the edge of that swamp, in a wood-frame house that my grandfather built from lumber the railroad had tossed away. While it was my home turf, little did I know what was ahead when the three of us got the idea to throw a few supplies into a twelve-foot boat and make our way toward the ocean, surviving on crawfish and berries along the way.

It wasn't long before the fun turned to fear. Our boat quickly spun out of control in the fast-moving creek—gator-filled waters, as it turned out. Flip the boat, and we'd be in big trouble. We managed to gain control and paddled our way to the swamp, where another danger met us—poisonous snakes. After a really big cottonmouth slithered by the boat, we floated along in silence—what we'd gotten ourselves into began to sink in, but there was no turning back.

We decided to shortcut it to the Atlantic, so we left the main channel and headed for a denser marsh. Big mistake. The swamp can be like the Bermuda Triangle—it's easy to get lost and go in circles trying to find your way out. We were smart enough to bring along a compass, but that didn't keep us from spending an afternoon turning left, then right, then left, until we found our way back to the main channel.

When we weren't staring down death, we did have some fun. At one shallow point where there were no snakes or gators, we jumped out of the boat onto a peat moss carpet that was as bouncy as a trampoline—the reason the Creek Indians call the swamp the Land of Trembling Earth.

But nights on that trip were scary. We camped on a sandbar under our overturned boat. There in the dark, in that flimsy shelter, amid the friendly sounds of crickets and whip-poor-wills, were mysterious noises that left us imagining the worst (gators sliding in and out of the water, for one). After two sleepless nights, we finally paddled out into the St. Mary's River—the only thing that stood between us and the ocean. It was all we could do to keep the boat steady in that fast-moving, brackish water, but we were out of the swamp and our end goal—the Atlantic—was in sight. We'd finally made it.

CHOPPY ENTREPRENEURIAL WATERS

What does a two-day boat ride have to do with business? It was a lot like most entrepreneurial ventures. We had jumped in that boat and headed off on a whim. We had what, in our minds, was a great idea, but we had only a flimsy plan and took off with very little in the way of gear.

CROSS THE SWAMP

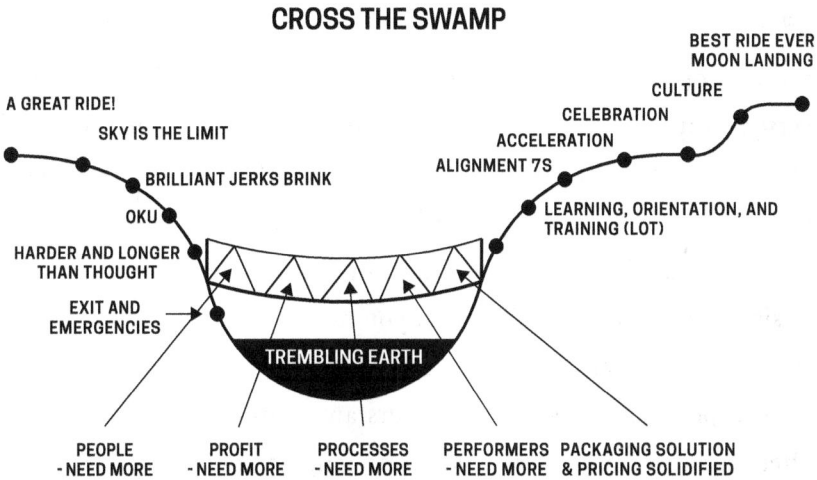

Figure 1

That's how most ventures start. Someone has a "great idea," puts up a shingle, and expects business to start rolling in (see figure 1). But before long, that person ends up in choppy waters. Or, that great idea actually takes off, but eventually ends up in deep water.

It's one thing to be successful when you're small, but fast growth is a different world. It's easy to make mistakes—sometimes costly mistakes. But that's what entrepreneurs do. They take off without knowing what's ahead because, let's face it, if they did, they might never start. If I had known how hard it was going to be for my nascent company to open an office in Hong Kong, I would never have done it. But after two years of misery and pain, we won a contract with

DHL—which kept the company afloat.

You see, I'm a fast-growth entrepreneur myself. My career started at UPS, where I developed a help desk system that, in its first year, saved the company more than $250 million. I left UPS to start STI Knowledge, an information technology company that made the *Inc. 500* list of the fastest-growing private companies in America three years in a row. When I sold STI Knowledge eight years later, it had offices in the US, Great Britain, South Africa, India, Hong Kong, and the Philippines. After selling the company, I endowed Emory University's top-ten-ranked executive MBA program and then founded the Oxford Center for Entrepreneurs, which helps entrepreneurs scale their businesses to join world-leading CEOs.

There is plenty of information out there about how to start a business. *Know Grow Exit* is what you need to know once the checks start rolling in, and when it's time for you to check out. I speak from experience: most entrepreneurs are ready to sell their venture after seven to twelve years. We don't tend to stay in a business for decades—we get bored too easily.

So how do you grow a company and have it ready to sell in as few as seven years? As a fast-growth entrepreneur, I know. And I'm sharing that with you in the pages ahead. If you're an entrepreneur who wants to *Know Grow Exit (KGE)*, then this book is for you.

KNOW

CHAPTER ONE

KNOW BEFORE GROWING A BUSINESS

'm lucky. I was only fifteen years old when I learned one of the most valuable business lessons any entrepreneur needs: *know your business.*

It happened when I joined my uncle Buddy in selling what we were sure was going to be overnight gold—Louisiana Pinks. No, I'm not talking about cosmetics or some frilly product. I'm talking about something every pond or river bottom-fisher needs—live worms. These aren't just any earthworms; they are the hardiest bait worms around. They're bigger and pinker and they stay alive on the hook longer than other worms. A tasty treat for the really big catfish and bream. They're not cheap, but they're worth every penny.

Uncle Buddy and I came across our winning idea when the local bait and tackle store, Winge's, upped the price of Pinks to a whopping $4 per box—twenty cents per Pink.

But while we may have been pretty good fishermen, running a worm business was something we knew nothing about. Still, when we found a wholesaler selling those fat worms at $2.25 per box, we figured we could undercut Winge's by charging $3 per box and it'd be the start of something really big. So we bought a refrigerator, filled it with fifty boxes of Pinks, put up our sign, and sat back and waited for the cash to roll in. After two days, we'd only sold two boxes (to my cousin Walter). Worse, we noticed that the wigglers still in the fridge had quit wiggling—and they were looking more pitiful by the hour.

We sped over to Winge's to check out their cooler and quickly figured out our problem. Our cooler was too cold. Upping the thermostat didn't fix the problem, so we pooled our money and bought another cooler, then patted ourselves on the back for being so quick to adjust.

That night, our first big sale showed up: two well-known fishermen pulled up and asked for four boxes of Pinks. I was so excited to fill their order that I broke the key off in the cooler door. Since they weren't going fishing until the next afternoon, we convinced them to return the next morning for their worms. At dawn, we were ready and waiting for our customers, but they never came back. (Hint: As a start-up, "waiting" is what you do when you don't know what else to do.) Not only that, but our twenty-to-a-box Pinks were quickly turning into fifteen to a box. Turns out, they were eating each other.

Clueless, we went back to Winge's to talk to the owner. Since he had such a big operation selling gas, beer, wine, snacks, and top-of-the-line fishing gear, we figured he'd be open to sharing tips with a couple of budding businessmen.

"I heard y'all were selling worms," he said. Opening a box of our worms and overturning them onto the truck bed, he started rattling off the rules of selling Pinks: you need five holes, not four, in the carton tops; the dirt is too dry—it needs to be misted; stop overfeeding them—they need to burrow for their food. Finally, he said, "I wish y'all would've asked me before you started. I carry those Pinks because nobody else around these parts will. I don't make much money on them, same as with the fishing licenses." You see, for Winge's, Pinks weren't profit-makers. Winge's only sold them as an add-on to sales of $100 fishing rods.

Later that day, Uncle Buddy gave away the cooler and every still-living Louisiana Pink inside. Our venture was a bust except for the one valuable lesson I learned: *know your business.*

THE VENTURE FARM

When you're just getting started in business, there is a stage that I call "venture farm." Successful entrepreneurs are not exploiters; they don't like to take big gambles. But starting a business takes more than vision and knowledge. It also takes a very particular kind of homework—you need to find out what people will write checks for. Nothing happens until you sell something: there's no money for the accountants to count, and there's no one for HR to hire. So you have to find ways to attract people to your business. That's the venture farm stage.

That starts by knowing the industry you're going to operate in. Sounds like a no-brainer, but a staggering number of businesses open every year simply because people think they have a great idea. There's a big difference between believing you have a great idea and actually *knowing* that you do.

Talking to people is one way of finding out who is going to write a check. But just getting feedback from friends and family isn't the best input to base a business on. If people think you have a great idea, ask them if they'll buy it. People will tell you if they'd buy a good idea. People will even prepay for an idea if they think it's outstanding. Before CNN went on the air, Ted Turner sold a lot of advertising. How? He went around talking up the twenty-four-hour news channel he was starting. It was a great idea, and people who knew it whipped out their checkbooks and bought advertising.

Also ask other business owners. Other entrepreneurs—often even competitors—will be surprisingly open about sharing the challenges they face. Every industry has hurdles, and every entrepreneur has war stories—and wins—that they are happy to talk about.

The best way to change an industry and create a new market is to know what is working now and which customers are being underserved. Companies often fail because they don't find their customer—that's because they think *everyone* is their customer. These are the entrepreneurs who go into business dead set on "pursuing their passion" without figuring out whether they have a product that anyone even wants. Pursuing your passion is overrated. No matter how much you may love the idea of going into business to chase your lifelong dream, on-the-job training is going to cost a lot more than learning who your customer is before you begin.

Take the failed meal kit company Chef'd—a venture that seemed to have everything going for it. Campbell's poured money into it. Smithfield Foods poured money into it. Investors poured money into it. The *New York Times* endorsed it. Chef'd looked like a slam dunk. But it never found its underserved customer.

Part of the venture farm stage is about finding and filling unmet needs. What product or service has the shortest sale cycle? What product can you sell that you don't have to discount? Figuring that out—fast—is the difference between a successful venture farm stage and an unsuccessful one.

Once the first check is cashed, and the product goes out the door, what's next? You've got to be ready to follow the best lead. What's gaining traction in the market? You may have gone into business selling to one type of customer, but pretty soon find another type wants to buy from you. You may build a base of customers in a niche you never expected, simply because you deliver when the competition can't. That's what happened to Mark Segal, and he was quick to recognize it.

Segal knew waste management inside out, so he thought it'd be a cinch to build his own company. When he started out, like many entrepreneurs, he had ambitious plans: he was going to build a new, full-service, national waste-management company from the ground up.

When he opened for business, he offered dumpsters, portable toilets, and more. Whatever customers demanded, he tried to add it to the list. Before long, he noticed that a lot of customers needed same-day dumpsters and portable toilets—they didn't have time to wait two weeks for a delivery. Construction sites needed a dumpster *today*. Schools with plumbing emergencies needed portable toilets *today*. And no other supplier was meeting those needs. No one else offered same-day deliveries.

Another plus of Segal's customers? They were willing to pay a premium price. Once Segal figured that out and focused on that winning niche, then his business really took off.

Entrepreneurs want to change the world. *Successful* entrepreneurs change the world for their target customer within their niche. They know the key to growing and finishing fast is to stay in your lane—focus on your niche and don't get distracted by shiny objects. Thanks to Mark Segal recognizing that, the world changed for the elementary school administrator who suddenly needed thirty portable toilets because the plumbing went kaput.

YOU'LL NEED A COMPASS

There's a reason the venture farm stage has such a high fatality rate: It can take time and a lot of changing direction to figure out that sweet spot where you enter hypergrowth—just when you have few resources to work with.

After I founded my technology company, STI Knowledge, there were months when the whole thing could have gone under. If it wasn't for a little smoke and mirrors, we probably *would* have sunk. At one point, when the company employed nine people, we were bidding on a $3.2 million contract for American Business Products and going up against none other than IBM.

When bidding on a contract of that size, IBM usually brought along a dozen people. So, I brought the *entire* company to the meeting with Ron Ford, ABP's CFO. We were a motley crew, dressed in suits that were either way too big or too small, but we were confident in our product—I may have been more confident than anyone in the room. When Ford asked questions about our software, I answered yes to every one—even if our software at that moment couldn't do what he asked. You see, I figured the features he needed could be added by the time the contract would actually go into effect.

The more he asked, the more I said yes, the bigger my team's eyes got (although no one piped up and said no). It was such a crucial time in the company's growth that the only acceptable answer was yes. Had I said no, we would have folded. Ultimately, STI Knowledge did make it. By the time I exited, 87 percent of Fortune 500 companies would use our product.

Smoke and mirrors helped STI go from nine motley suits to serving most of the Fortune 500. When you're in venture farm stage, you'll need a little smoke and mirrors. You'll need a compass.

The rest of this book is that compass.

NEW BUSINESS GROWTH STAGES

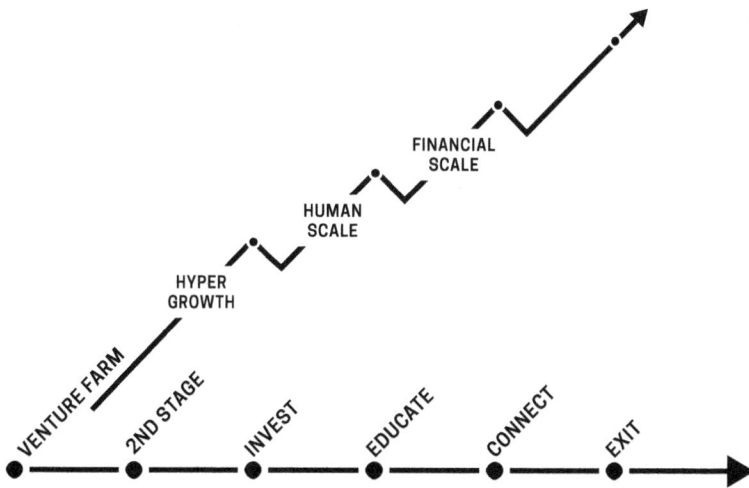

Figure 2: The stages of a new business

The venture farm stage is about finding and filling unmet needs where you can charge above-market pricing. When my motley crew of nine staffers went up against IBM for a $3.2 million contract, we weren't really trying to become the next IBM. We were trying to become *the* brand name in our niche. In that niche, we could charge higher margins than the industry standard. Same with Mark Segal. He became the IBM of instant waste-management solutions, and healthy margins followed.

Once you figure out your niche, then you start growing—fast. That's the hypergrowth stage. The next section of this book is devoted to what you need to know during hypergrowth, along with the next two stages of any fast-growth business: human scale and financial scale (see figure 2).

Then I'll talk about your *exit*. As an entrepreneur, the best time to plan your exit is before you start. That's right: you should launch your company with an end in mind. Yet, nobody wants to be one of the 82 percent of entrepreneurs who are unhappy about their decision to sell one year after they're out of the business. KGE entrepreneurs know how to spot their peak exit opportunity, get the maximum price, and be happy about their decision.

Let's start by helping you navigate through the first fast-growth stage: hypergrowth.

SECTION II

GROW

CHAPTER TWO

SURVIVING HYPERGROWTH

n the venture farm stage, entrepreneurs are out there pounding the pavement, trying to find that underserved customer and figuring out what people will pay them for. Once you find your underserved customer and capture your niche, you enter hypergrowth.

Hypergrowth is the fun stage. Now you've got your market, people are writing you checks, and your venture is taking off. In this fast-growth stage, it's tempting to feel like the sky is the limit.

But the real numbers are sobering. For every ten companies that reach $1 million, fewer than two make it to $2 million. That's because they don't reach the next stage of fast growth: human scale. In KGE lingo, human scale occurs when a company can finally produce its hundredth widget for less than its ninety-ninth. That is, when you've reached human scale, increasing volume adds more to revenue than it does to expenses. In the next few chapters, I'll talk about what it takes to make it through hypergrowth to that level of achievement known as human scale.

One of the first things you'll need to know is what a childhood neighbor of mine grasped early on in his venture: make work fun.

J. D. Harris was a farmer who lived nearby. At the end of the harvest season, he was tasked with killing the rats that took over his corncribs. Over time, it became a task he couldn't handle on his own, so he posted a help-wanted sign out by the road offering cash to anyone who showed up on Saturday to help him kill the rats.

The first Saturday he tried the tactic was a bust; not a single soul showed up to help him kill rats. Why? Because killing rats is a heinous job. No amount of money was going to attract the hands Harris needed.

The next Saturday, however, was a different story. My brother Kenny and I watched as a long line of trucks parked along the road and troves of people piled out and headed over to our neighbor's farm. What had changed in that one week? His approach to recruiting. Instead of just offering cash for kills, he'd turned a chore into a festival.

To attract the hands he needed to his farm, Harris decided to make a game of killing rats. He built a huge bonfire—thirty feet tall—and passed out spears that he'd made and dressed up with feathers; special tools designed just for killing rats. Then, as a reward for the hunter who killed the most rats, he offered what many around those parts considered the best of prizes: a Zebco One fishing reel with a graphite rod.

That rod and reel, a thirty-foot bonfire, and the chance to get primitive with a spear drew people from one hundred miles away.

MAKE WORK FUN

Work is demanding in a fast-growth environment—so demanding that there's a real danger of burnout. People don't last in a fast-growth company unless they enjoy what they're doing.

That's why the idea worked—Harris knew that a challenge like getting people to help with a repulsive task could be overcome if he made the work fun. His idea was such a good one that he held that festival for years after that.

I see companies all the time trying to create "fun" workplaces to keep their people happy and on the job. But I'm not talking about exercises like lunchtime ping-pong or Friday-afternoon paintball scrimmages as "fun" team building. Those are big wastes of time and money.

What I'm talking about is the work itself. It's a little like software: if users *like* using it, then it's more likely to succeed. If not, then it's probably headed for the trash bin.

Making work fun is essential for a fast-growth company. For companies like Zappos, making work fun made a name for the company. And that showed up quickly in the bottom line. The online shoe and clothing retailer is renowned for its cool, smart, fast culture. But long before it built that reputation, company leaders had to figure out how to get shoes out the door—fast—to keep customers happy and to outdo the competition. And they had to do it without losing employees in the process. The solution? Hire people, a whole team of people, who wanted to work at that fast pace—and do it with a smile.

As soon as your business is more than an idea, you're going to need a team of people who can get the work done the way it needs to be done. Having the *right* people on the team makes all the difference between success and failure.

Sometimes that means sending away people who just don't fit. When J. D. Harris threw his festival, my brother and I strolled over to check it out, even though our dad told us to stay away. We weren't there to kill rats—we just wanted to see what all the fuss was about. Harris knew we didn't fit in. He knew we'd spoil the fun for everyone else, so he sent us home as soon as he saw us. The same is true in business. If you don't get rid of the people who don't fit, the ones who aren't having fun, they can ruin what you're trying to do. They can ruin it for everyone.

Believe me, there's always a way to make work fun. When I worked in technology at UPS, the drivers spent a few minutes socializing before heading out in their trucks. They spent their days driving around all alone in their trucks, delivering packages. But those few minutes in the morning made the day's work more fun. It wasn't anything fancy (no ping-pong table in sight); it was just folks milling around, shooting the breeze over coffee.

DEFINING CULTURE

What you're doing when building your team is building a culture. Despite what you may read, or what a consultant may tell you, a culture is not something that you can concoct. It's not something you can just reconstruct overnight either.

Recently, I was an adviser in the sale of a fast-growth company to a huge, public corporation. The first day after the sale, a scrappy HR person from the bigger corporation showed up and told everyone to come outside. Handing each person a balloon filled with helium, she shouted, "Release—and let go of your old culture!" The idea was that the old culture would somehow float away on the breeze and a new culture would take its place—just like that.

Wanting to know more, over lunch, I asked the HR person to define "culture." She launched into a long-winded, HR-speak answer before saying, "I don't think you can ever define what a company culture is. It's a journey that has no end."

Wrong.

Simply put, culture is *how the work gets done.*

Zappos is a great example because it clearly shows the links between the work, the people, and the culture. That's how culture happens: the work first, then the people, then the culture. Zappos built the team to get the work done, and the result is a winning company known for its culture.

That is one of your most important jobs as the leader of a fast-growth company: to build the team that can do the work and that thrives on a fast pace.

So where do you find these superhumans? Start by understanding what they're like. People who thrive in a fast-growth workplace tend to have certain primal work instincts.

They have good judgment. A lot of articles on building a team say to look for employees with good judgment. Fast-growth companies need to go a step further—your employees need the primal instinct of *fast-growth* good judgment. They don't just show up for work ready to be told what to do. They show up with a sense of what needs to be done, without being told. And then they do it.

They are naturally curious. Fast-growth teams aren't satisfied with the status quo. They're always seeking out new information and they crave knowing what's outside their comfort zone. They avoid boredom, so you might find them at the Russian opera and NASCAR in the same weekend looking not for entertainment, but trying to understand how such venues captivate an audience.

They value communication. Fast-growth employees know how to communicate clearly no matter the chaos around them. They maintain calm in times of stress, and they know how to quickly make sense of any situation. Instead of wasting time being alarmed, they pick up the pieces and keep moving. At the same time, they know how to motivate and teach others.

They're selfless. They share information openly and proactively—they know how and when to speak up instead of holding back. They're happiest when they're giving more than they're taking.

They passionately solve problems. The workers you need in a fast-growth environment are about more than just cheers and tears. Instead of just treating symptoms, they look for the root cause of a problem and go after a solution for that.

They don't fear failure. Knowing that desperation drives innovation, fast-growth workers keep trying and aren't afraid to fail. In fact, they view failure as an opportunity to figure out how to succeed.

They have the courage to deal with conflict. Fast-growth staffers have the courage to object when the company is going in a direction that conflicts with its values. But they also know to keep pushing ahead toward success even when they disagree with a tactical or day-to-day decision.

They want to make an impact. When the company has a need, that's when fast-growth workers come through. They don't hide—they're the ones who want the ball when the game is on the line.

They do what's right—even when no one is looking. Fast-growth workers are honest. They admit mistakes and do what's right without having to be called out.

You can hire for skills and train people to do necessary tasks. You can even shape the team's personality to align with what's needed to win in your market. But what you can't do is train, shape, or change the primal work instincts that people need to match the dynamics of a fast-growth company.

Your people are your path to a positive culture. The traits I've described are what you need in a fast-growth company. When you find these traits in people, hire them, onboard them, and challenge them to change the world—and give them the space to do so.

I'll talk more about hiring—and firing—people in the chapters ahead. First, let's look at the blueprint for fast growth, what's known as the McKinsey 7S Framework.

THE MCKINSEY 7S FRAMEWORK—A BLUEPRINT FOR FAST GROWTH

In the hypergrowth stage, fast-growth businesses tend to be mired in chaos: they may be changing the market segment they're serving, adjusting their product mix, juggling roles, changing employees, organizing and reorganizing. Pretty much everything is in flux.

The key to succeeding as a fast-growth company is to manage all that chaos. That's the difference between fast and slow companies—slow companies get lost or run over in the mix.

The McKinsey 7S Framework (see figure 3 on the following page) is a tool for creating stability, a blueprint that focuses on organizational alignment and accelerating organic growth. Its elements include shared values, style, skills, staff, strategy, structure, and systems.

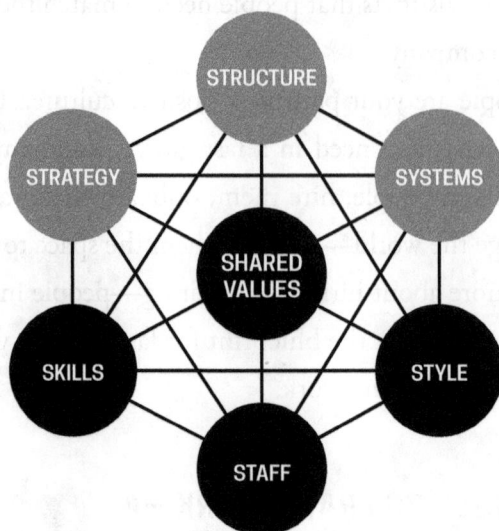

Figure 3

SHARED VALUES

At the core of the McKinsey 7S Framework are shared values. A fast-growth company's shared values explicitly state why the company exists. They are the fundamental beliefs that underlie the culture of the organization—they guide its decisions and behaviors and set the company apart. To determine shared values, just ask: "Why do we exist?"

A prime example of shared values was UPS's statement during its brutal expansion years that the US economy depended on the company moving commerce from point A to point B. With that kind of responsibility on its shoulders, the UPS team absolutely had to be successful. That's sharing a set of values.

Southwest cofounder and former CEO Herb Kelleher also understood the power of shared values. He grounded his company in them by emphasizing that Southwest's purpose was to help families have more time together by moving them from point A to point B via air travel versus bus. Kelleher knew that motivating baggage handlers to load suitcases onto airplanes in the pouring rain would take more than money—they would need to see themselves as helping families spend time together. He built a winning company by ensuring that every member of the team shared the same values.

For some companies, values are only words chiseled on a wall. They're not an underlying set of beliefs that guides decisions and behaviors. That was the case with Enron, an energy giant turned epic failure.

At one point, Enron was a client of my growing tech company, STI Knowledge. The first time I walked into the Enron headquarters, I paused to admire the impressive lobby. There, chiseled in the marble walls, were nice-sounding values: Honesty, Integrity, Community, Respect, and Excellence. Admittedly, I was a little humbled by what appeared to be a remarkable company. But that impression didn't last long.

There was something curious about the way their teams operated. One of the ways to get ahead at Enron was to poach employees from other departments. That's how people moved up in Enron, and how they netted promotions—basically, they were rewarded for stealing from each other. No matter what was chiseled into the walls, Enron's culture valued stealing.

Make no mistake: Enron's culture of stealing didn't happen overnight. It developed from the people who were hired and promoted. And those chiseled words were likely the product of a group gathered around a conference table to decide the "values" that the company wanted to advertise. They were not formed by asking "Why do we exist?"

Your company's shared values are who you really are—not who you want to be, or who you want your customers or investors to think you are. Shared values are a higher calling, something that can motivate the team to keep pushing forward when the going gets rough. They are the reason you come to work every day.

STYLE

Style is how the business gets work done and how it appears to the world. In hypergrowth, your company may be known as easy to do business with, in part, because it has an open management style. That's different from large corporations, which are typically a mishmash of styles: slow and methodical accounting, fast and sloppy sales, a cocky C-suite, and middle managers too scared to take action.

Your style will affect your business systems. If your style is fast, then your systems won't involve a lot of details that bog down processes. It will also affect the type of people you hire: fast accountants, fast salespeople, and fast leaders. In other words, if you're a fast company, then your style is to be fast across the organization.

Style helps a company find and keep a rhythm—an important ingredient for growth. Having a distinctive style makes work fun—and makes the company easier to scale.

SKILLS

The skills your team needs depend on your industry and company. All companies need two types of skills: internal skills that allow individuals to succeed within the company, and external skills that allow the company as a whole to maintain a competitive advantage over the competition.

As you're building your team, you will need to hire with both types of skills in mind. Consider this excerpt from a real job posting by an Oxford Center member:

> *We're looking for someone to fit into our fast-paced culture—someone with a strong understanding of the world of ideas, and a keen interest in what's hot, what's happening, and what's relevant to employees and clients. The ideal candidates are voracious readers, curious, and Get Stuff Done fanatics. But also—we can't stress this enough—they are people with amazing sales skills internally and externally. Candidates must be familiar with, and excel at, the sales process. You must be able to understand and sell intangibles, and be tenacious, persistent, and persuasive, on the phone and by email. You must be able to get attention, and hold it, in a helpful and authentic manner.*
>
> *The job is hard, but it's also fun and meaningful work. You need to be able to prospect, maintain and grow a client base, to guide a sale from beginning to end, manage expectations, meet quotas, engage fully with projects hanging in the balance between done and not done and to speak—with clarity, purpose, and verve—about our roster of industry-changing projects.*

Most of the post emphasizes the *qualities* that a person needs to bring to the team. That, combined with the hard skills needed for the job, will help you build a team with the skills your venture needs to thrive during hypergrowth.

STAFF

Historically, some of the lowest-paid people in a business are those who deal with customers. Their positions are viewed as low skill, so their pay is typically near the bottom of the scale.

But fast growth dictates building a team that is excited enough to fulfill your mission, even if you can't offer the pay that established companies can.

Southwest's Herb Kelleher understood that. He paid top dollar to his gate agents to attract great people who would solve customers' problems. At Southwest, customer service became a competitive advantage.

Starbucks did something similar. Baristas historically made poor wages until Starbucks began offering better pay and a work environment that would attract an army of enthusiastic, competent people to serve its customers.

STRATEGY

The business world is papered with lengthy philosophies on corporate strategy. During fast growth, the definition of strategy is simple: *Strategy is doing a different set of activities, in a different way, from the competition.*

Your strategy must lay out how the company creates value for customers in a way that sets it apart. Is the strategy to deliver a product in less time than anyone else (remember Mark Segal in chapter 1)? Is it to offer a time-saving product that costs less? That's how Southwest set itself apart—with a point-to-point system that was different than the hub-and-spoke model of competitors.

STRUCTURE

There's a fear in fast-growth companies that a lack of structure or a flat hierarchy will lead to chaos. While you don't need the kind of layered hierarchy found at a huge corporation, you do need a framework for who does what.

Netflix CEO Reed Hastings has called the best structure for an entrepreneurial, high-growth enterprise "highly aligned and loosely coupled." In this structure, the strategy and goals are debated and defined, and then the team is trusted to execute tactics without having to gain approvals in advance. When an issue arises, the team evaluates what happened, and then does a reset. It's a structure that involves a lot of shared values, trust, and transparency, and it requires a team of high performers who are given the freedom to fail, and then try again.

SYSTEMS

When a company is in its early stages, only the founder and perhaps another team member may have most of the company's knowledge in their head(s). Or, it may be jotted down on napkins or stuck on computer monitors with Post-its. To scale the company, you must create systems that every new hire can follow.

Figure 4 exemplifies the importance and impact of exiting your company. Each category has challenges and hurdles that you'll need to overcome as the company scales and becomes more complex (as the company grows from venture farm to hypergrowth to human scale to financial scale). Once you are aware of these stages leading up to exit, you can plan to exit earlier.

HOW SYSTEMS CHANGE AS THE COMPANY SCALES

AREA OF FOCUS	VENTURE FARM	HYPERGROWTH	HUMAN SCALE	FINANCIAL SCALE
REVENUE RANGE	$0-10M	$10-30M	>$30M	<$50B
STRUCTURE OF ORGANIZATION	Informal—managed by founders	Simple base management team	Formal leadership team	Complex/ hierarchical structure with C-suite
GROWTH OBJECTIVES	Adopting business lines/markets	Distribution network/sales team	Multistate, targeted international/ bolt-on M&A	Global consolidator
PRODUCT DEVELOPMENT	Prototypes/R&D/ trial production runs	QC/R&D/ leveraged manufacturing	Quality/R&D/ central manufacturing	QC/R&D/ multiple production plants
FINANCING SOURCES	Founders/venture /friends/angel, reverse merger	Founders/venture/ mezzanine/banks	Banks, customers	PE/banks/IPO/ equity
ACCOUNTING SYSTEMS/ CONTROLS	Basic systems	OTC systems, practical controls	Customized, formal systems	Sophisticated systems and controls
ACCOUNTING ISSUES	Capitalization vs. expense start-ups	Controls/segregation of duties	Cash planning to finance growth	Technical position papers
	Recording of equity transactions	Revenue recognition	Goodwill vs. separate ident intangible	Corporate internal audit department support
	Capturing all transactions timely	Equity transactions and options	Inventory methods (LIFO/FIFO)	Financial disclosures
	Unaudited financial statements	Audited reviews	Reserves, valuations, audited financial statements	SEC reporting
	Cash flow projections / burn rate	Debt agreements/ covenants	Strategic partnerships	International financial reporting standards
	Basic record keeping with support	Technical accounting assistance	Variable interest entities (FIN 46)	Accounting avoidance
	Cash vs. accrual accounting	Financial statement disclosures	SOX controls and practices	Mergers JVs due diligence
		Accounting for intangibles/IP	International operations/ transactions	Consultants M&A buy side

Figure 4: Systems change as a company scales.

Systems aren't only necessary in finance, accounting, or manufacturing. Sales and marketing must also be systemized. But those are areas that can be especially tough to manage. In the chapters ahead, I'll talk about sales and marketing, and I'll talk more about creating the team that you need for fast growth. Before I go any further, let me first share with you why it's best to resist the temptation to hire the "dream team" when it comes to leaders.

HIGH LEVEL VERSUS HIGH PERFORMING— THERE'S A DIFFERENCE

During fast growth, it's tempting to want to hire leaders with big titles from large companies. Bad idea. There is a fundamental difference between high-level and high-performing leaders.

At one point when I was growing STI Knowledge, I hired a CFO with an impressive résumé to help clean up some massive accounting issues. He came in and resolved those with clarity and function, so I thought that hiring a "dream team" of national sales leaders would be a good next step. Everything seemed fine for a couple of weeks, but then the problems began.

It started when I noticed a large receivable on the books from a Fortune 50 company. I asked the new CFO about the unpaid account; in fact, I asked him several times. But each time I asked, he'd pass the buck. "I'll have Mattie call them," he'd say. In the meantime, the unpaid bill kept growing. When the account topped $140,000, I asked the CFO to make the call himself to get the receivable resolved.

"You want me to make a collections call?" he asked. He didn't think collections were part of his job. He was a high-level employee and didn't know what it meant to be high performing. In other words, he wasn't great at "doing." He wasn't someone who could work in the trenches in the morning, talk to CEOs of major corporations in the afternoon, and rally the troops in the evening.

Similar things were happening with the new sales heavy hitters I had hired. For the first two weeks, they had a lot of opinions for what the rest of the team could do to improve operations. They showed that they had the "walking around" authority to discuss their domain and general company business. But like the CFO, they weren't great at "doing." In fact, they were baffled as to why they had to make their own copies when we had people who could do it for them.

When hiring high-level people for your team, you need professionals who can also perform at the pace hypergrowth demands. As Laura Zander, CEO of Jimmy Beans Wool, has said: "High-level people come with high-level problems." High-level employees tend to have high expectations about how they will be treated. Instead of understanding the urgency of growth, they tend to be more like actors who demand high pay and need a supporting cast.

A highly successful corporate executive once told me, "I never make a decision where I can be blamed, but I am always in the room when the decision is made, so I can be there to celebrate success." An attitude like that will sink a fast-growth company where it's all about *how the work gets done.*

Instead of seeking out big names, consider these when hiring leaders for your team:

- overachievers within your own company

- rising stars in your industry

- customers who are highly committed to your cause

- friends of your overachieving staff

I'll talk more about these in the chapters ahead. For now, as you're looking to hire leaders, remember to determine whether they have the primal work instincts I mentioned earlier and whether they are "doers" who are aligned with your company's shared values, style, and strategy.

GETTING INTO ALIGNMENT— SOMETIMES YOU HAVE TO SAY NO

It used to be that people working for the airlines wore dark polyester uniforms with shiny metal buttons. But that didn't really reflect the style of Southwest Airlines. Instead, Southwest's style became Bermuda shorts and tennis shoes. On the first day that Southwest crews showed up in that attire, security staff mistook them for tourists and wouldn't let them in the door. By 2003—after three decades in operation—Southwest had become the largest domestic carrier in the United States.

What CEO Herb Kelleher had achieved was alignment. In addition to the shared values, setting the company apart as a low-cost point-to-point carrier, and prioritizing the value of customer service and rewarding staff for providing it with better pay, he visually aligned the company in a way that was different than the norm. Inside and out, every element of the company was in alignment.

That alignment was the product not only of all the things Southwest chose *to* do, but also what it chose *not* to do. Kelleher chose to target low-cost, family fliers, which meant saying no to luxury amenities—those would not have been in alignment with the rest of the operation or with Southwest's demographic.

Saying no can be a difficult lesson for an entrepreneur, but it's essential for alignment. You've got to remember to stay focused on your niche, and avoid those shiny objects. Steve Jobs once said, "I'm actually as proud of the things we *haven't* done as the things we have done. Innovation is saying 'no' to 1,000 things."[1] I learned that the hard way.

When STI Knowledge was in hypergrowth, it was innovating across the board: engineering had a new platform, programming had new features, marketing had new campaigns, and the sales department wanted to split the team into old and new products. In other words, there were too many unfinished "innovations" in the pipeline that weren't bringing in much-needed revenue. The team had simply grown long on excuses and short on results.

Fed up, I finally stood up in one excruciating late-night staff meeting and declared: "Nobody else in this company can make something new unless it's approved by me. Everyone needs to go and do what we already said we were going to do. Finish it or eliminate it—your decision." No more talking—it was time for "doing."

They knew I meant it. They went back to their desks and started executing. That's why, at times, during the hypergrowth stage, you've got to learn to say no. When fast growth starts to fade, as it will, the problem is rarely innovation. Usually, it's an inability to do what follows innovation—getting stuff done. That means making, packaging, selling, delivering, and collecting the money to increase revenue and profits. The biggest risk to a fast-growth business is not that it will die because it stops innovating—it's that it will die because you don't rein in all the innovating and start executing.

It all goes back to the culture definition I shared at the beginning of the chapter: *It's how the work gets done.* It's easy to tell what a company's culture is by who's been fired and who's been promoted.

---

1   "Steve Jobs: Innovation Is Saying 'No' to 1,000 Things," Zurb, https://zurb.com/blog/steve-jobs-innovation-is-saying-no-to-1-0.

At Enron, the people who were great at stealing got promoted. At my company, we eliminated people who couldn't keep up with the pace, and we promoted those who were doers and found the work exhilarating. Since our style was fast, our culture was fast. That's how we got results.

Still, even I didn't understand how everything had to align to fast style and culture until I was the one out of alignment.

When trying to sell our product to Fortune 500 customers, we regularly made it to the last round of bidding for even the most highly competitive contracts. But we kept coming in second without landing the contract. Second is the worst position because it involves the heavy expense of the sales cycle but none of the revenue of the win. I was certain that we had the best solution at the best price, and it always seemed like the C-suite was leaning in our direction. But after the "socialization period" to decide which of the final two contenders they were going to partner with, potential customers always seemed to choose our competition.

At first, I blamed our losses on being a new company. Finally, I figured out the problem—*I wasn't the image of success.*

I was showing up to the appointments in a Ford Bronco. There was nothing wrong with its appearance other than the fact that it wasn't the type of vehicle that a problem-solver should emerge from—no Fortune 500 executives want to hear that they have a problem, and they certainly don't want any problem they have to be solved by a guy driving a Bronco.

I swapped out the black Bronco for a BMW 740. I also revised my pitch. Instead of telling potential clients they had problems, I told them they had great visions but needed help from the right technology partner.

Those two actions flipped us into alignment and led to incredible growth.

Make no mistake: If I were in the business of selling Louisiana Pinks, pulling up in a BMW would have blown every sale. The key is to create the right alignment throughout your company for your particular values and market.

CHAPTER THREE

YOUR BUSINESS IS AN ECOSYSTEM

Swamps are delicate ecosystems. During floods, the swamp basin swells as it takes on more water. During droughts, it releases that water into rivers and creeks. During severe droughts, the peat moss that makes up the spongy swamp floor can dry up and become flammable—light a match, and it can all go up in smoke.

Fast-growth businesses are also fragile ecosystems. One wrong move, and the whole thing can disappear in a cloud of smoke. That's why entrepreneurs must tend to their business ecosystem—it's the only way to survive hypergrowth and move into what's known as human scale.

At their core, all businesses are technical in nature. It's not that you shouldn't be passionate about being in business for yourself. As I mentioned in chapter 1, pursuing your passion is overrated. Passion is less a predictor of success than is technical expertise. A Yale University study found that viewing your passion as a single, fixed entity—as opposed to something that evolves, and that you discover in an ongoing process—makes it more likely that you'll quit when that so-called passion ebbs.[2] Instead of viewing passion as a single magic bullet for success, focus on what you know—that is, the technical expertise needed to grow your business.

When I left UPS in 1995 to begin building STI Knowledge, I wasn't following a passion. I didn't make the leap suddenly, and I didn't do it alone. While working in the UPS technology department, I identified the need for the product that we would go on to build at STI. Long before I gave up my UPS paycheck, my colleagues and I spent time kicking around the idea. When we were finally certain that our idea should be a business, a group of us left UPS and set up shop in a building a few blocks away. We started our venture on a foundation of technical expertise that we had developed together over time.

Interestingly, start-ups that have the highest success rate are those founded by a group of people who left a larger company together. Besides being a training ground, the larger company often ends up providing an invaluable pool of human capital once the new venture hits a growth phase. That was certainly true for STI; the first fifty people I hired were from UPS.

Still, even starting out with such assets, navigating hypergrowth is a feat.

---

2   Ephrat Livni, "'Find Your Passion' Is Bad, Say Yale and Stanford Psychologists," Yahoo Finance, June 26, 2018, accessed December 15, 2018, https://finance. yahoo.com/news/passion-bad-advice-yale-stanford-185038265.html.

HYPERGROWTH TO HUMAN SCALE—A STEEP CLIMB

In hypergrowth, you're identifying and building shared values, style, skills, staff, strategy, structure, and systems. You're taking what you learned in the venture farm stage, and honing it into a fast-paced company that delivers as promised.

At some point in that hypergrowth incline, you'll find yourself in a treacherous place. The company will outgrow its infrastructure and you'll have to invest in better systems from top to bottom or the business will fold under the pressure of its own success.

NEW BUSINESS GROWTH STAGES

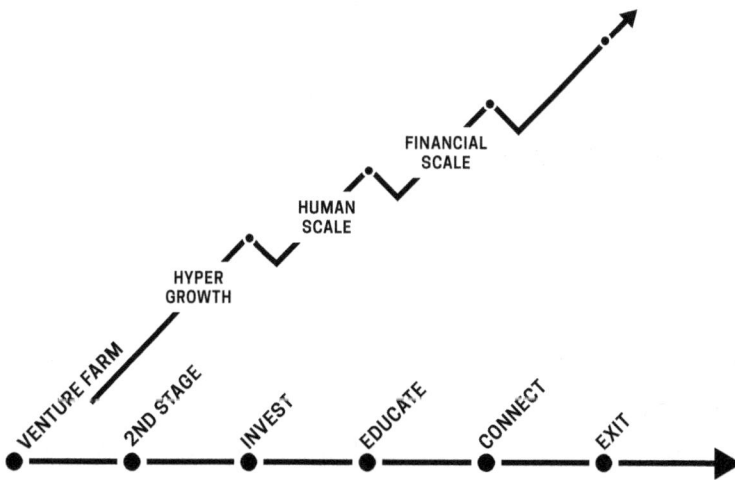

Figure 5: New business growth stages

For a while, you'll feel the pinch in your bottom line as those investments cut into profitability. That is actually a good thing: it means you're doing the right things to create sustainable profit—and it means you're transitioning to the next stage of growth, known as human scale.

No matter your industry or your company, every successful, growing business must endure the painful transition from hypergrowth to human scale, something that I think is important to reiterate here from chapter 1 (see figure 5). When you finally reach human scale, adding people improves profitability. You can start smiling every time the company makes a new hire, instead of worrying that you won't make payroll—because another person equals more profit.

Only one company in history went from hypergrowth to financial scale without reaching human scale first, and that company wound up paying a price for it.

That company was Uber. Since Uber's business operates on smartphones, it was able to go straight from hypergrowth to financial scale. But that would harm the company later, when its management team blatantly lacked the expertise necessary to steer a ship of that size.

Here are some ways to keep your business ecosystem in balance as you move through hypergrowth to human scale.

DO MORE WITH LESS

Earlier in the book, I rejected complex explanations of *culture* and *strategy* in favor of definitions that get to the heart of what it means to be an entrepreneur.

Now let me do the same for "entrepreneurship": *do more with less*.

When you're building a company, it's easy to be stymied by the constant need for more resources. You need more people, more data, more computers, more software, and more space. But until you reach the human scale stage, you must figure out how to get everything done with the skeletal resources you have.

Take Dr. Mark McKenna, an emerging real estate entrepreneur in New Orleans until Hurricane Katrina wiped his growing, fifty-person company off the map. Instead of giving up, he moved to

Atlanta and opened up a single-shingle wellness spa that he eventually sold to a $2 billion publicly traded fitness juggernaut. Along the way, McKenna stuck to his belief that the masses wanted access to spa-like wellness, and he used low-cost advertising tactics that best targeted his audience. I'll tell you more about McKenna's exit in chapter 9.

The way he ran his company is the essence of entrepreneurship. If you can figure out how to do more with less at every turn, then you're more likely to build a sustainable ecosystem.

THE MYTH OF THE "EARLY ADOPTER"

Earlier I told you the story of STI's start, when we were competing with IBM and, to tilt the scale, I told American Business Products' CFO that our team could do anything his company needed. That's necessary sometimes when starting a business.

But in business as a whole, there's a lie that's been told so long and so loudly that people accept it as fact. That's what I call a "whopper strategy."

In business, that whopper strategy is the myth of the "early adopter." According to this myth, there is always a group of business customers with an innate willingness and desire to be the first to try new products and services. Early adopters may exist on the consumer side of business—there are always a few techies who can't wait to try the latest gadget. But on the business side, it's dangerous to generalize that pattern. The early adopter theory says that there's a natural market out there just waiting for your product, and all you need to do is go out looking for buyers.

That's not how it works. I sold to Fortune 1000 customers for eight years and never came across one early adopter—for the simple reason that they don't exist.

The lie of the early adopter undermines the role of business founders and salespeople. Successful founders are really good at wheeling and dealing. They're good at selling, or getting other people to buy into their vision, and they're good negotiators who can even drive new market reality by dealing with give-and-take. Their customers who buy early versions of a new product aren't doing so because they're early adopters. They buy because they've encountered a founder who really *sells*.

In the B2B world, successful entrepreneurs sell new products and services by targeting agile organizations in a state of flux, rather than ones with a clearly defined problem looking for a predetermined solution. They also find change agents with budgets, rather than friendly informants who do not have purchasing authority. They are creative with requests for proposal (RFPs), but also show up with a plan B, an entirely different solution than on the RFP, because they're good at identifying and solving problems the client didn't even anticipate.

Don't fall into the trap of believing in the early adopter—there is no 14 percent of the market waiting to buy your innovations, in spite of what early adopter theorists would have you believe. If you go around looking for early adopters, you're going to come up empty-handed.

Instead, you must get out there with a great product and know how to sell it. That's how STI Knowledge made successful sales to 86 percent of Fortune 1000 companies, none of which was an early adopter. These companies were jumping on the bandwagon because we were burning up the market with a great product that we knew how to sell.

PERSONAL "BALANCE": EASIER SAID THAN DONE

When entrepreneurs are out there burning up the market, they want to apply that same high across their lives, but too often find themselves coming up short on the personal side. "How can fast-growth entrepreneurs lead a more balanced life?" That's one of the most agonizing questions that I'm asked. The answer is simple: they can't.

Fast growth is a 24/7 proposition. It's not just the hours you put in at work; the business owns your head. Work is on your mind in the shower, on vacation, while eating dinner, and when trying to help the kids with their homework. That can be disastrous to the big three—family, health, and faith. As F. Scott Fitzgerald said, "Show me a hero and I'll write you a tragedy." Entrepreneurs have the audacity to want to create or change a market, or just plain change the world. Once they smell success, it's hard to stop. They become a kind of addict—work is their "high."

I vividly remember when my HR director called me into her office one evening. She told me work had become my life. I blew off her warning because the business had taken off and I was having a great time. Since I also very much loved my family, I assumed I could balance it all. But dealing with routine matters at home (changing diapers, taking out the trash, going to homeowners' association meetings) was so slow paced that it bordered on tedium—hardly an equal level of excitement to the workplace.

Five years later, I had three Inc. 500 plaques hanging on my wall—and I was divorced.

There is scientific proof that entrepreneurs thrive on the insanity of long hours and long odds. I once hired a doctor with an MBA to explain to a group of CEOs the science of how the brain makes decisions and reacts to pleasures and failures. Dr. Dragana Bugarski showed us brain scans of heroin addicts, people engaged in intimate acts, people with attention deficit disorder, and entrepreneurs. Her presentation showed us that entrepreneurs get their drive and capacity for work fulfillment from the same brain stimulants that drive heroin addicts. The brain's pleasure center, she explained, drives entrepreneurs to stay late at work rather than go home. I still remember the thrill I got when IT called me after hours and said, "We are up and live in Hong Kong. South Africa is next." *That's* my drug.

Entrepreneurs think they want balance, but what they need if they are going to have a personal life is boundaries. For instance, you definitely can't make all of your daughter's softball games. But maybe you can attend a handful of games, and leave your phone in the car when you do. When you're with your family, be with them—resist the temptation to answer calls and emails. Boundaries are trade-offs, and entrepreneurs tend to be good at negotiating trade-offs. But trying to achieve "balance" is propaganda that will continue to perpetuate tragedies for the entrepreneur.

Fast growth means being all in, 24/7, for the mission and the success of the company. Today, as I consult with entrepreneurs, I advise them not to get married while they are in fast-growth mode. Bill Gates didn't get married until he was ready to exit as Microsoft's CEO.

Admittedly, holding off on building a family is difficult advice to follow for entrepreneurs who still want to believe that balance is possible.

In the middle of the twentieth century, when President John F. Kennedy spoke to this country about the space program's intention to put a man on the moon, he said something vitally important. He said that we go to the moon not because it's easy, but because it's hard.

Entrepreneurship is hard. It will also be one of the greatest rides of your life. If you are continually approaching it the way JFK approached the space program, with the idea that you're doing it precisely *because* it's hard, then you're on your way to success.

ON A MISSION—TOGETHER

Embracing a concept known as *oku* will serve you well when in hypergrowth and striving for human scale. *Oku* means giving a little more now to get a little more later. And you've got to *give* before you get. I saw *oku* in action when STI was desperately short on cash. Our CFO came to see me with what was supposed to be good news: with some belt-tightening measures, he said, we only had to lay off twelve or thirteen people. We looked at our list of team members and could find not a single person we thought was dispensable.

We had just made the list of the fastest-growing companies, meaning that our team had just delivered in a big way. I was adamant about not wanting to break the we-are-in-this-together bond. So instead of laying off a single person, I decided that the forty highest-paid people would take a 10 percent pay cut, and we would make up the rest in travel reductions.

I wasn't surprised when I didn't hear any whining, moaning, or groaning from the top forty—because there was a strong feeling that we were all on a mission together. But I *was* surprised when the person who would have been number forty-one came into my office and said he wanted to take the same pay cut. The next day, the HR director came to see me and said, "Cliff, I've had a stream of people in my office all day—team leaders, frontline people, just about every role—asking if they can take the 10 percent pay cut too. I don't even think we need the money."

I suppose I shouldn't have been surprised that the rest of the team wanted to be part of this pay cut that was going to serve as a bridge through a difficult financial stretch. This was *oku* in action: We put ourselves after the company. We put the company first. We were on a mission together.

Still, the fast-growth environment is brutal, and it's easy for burnout to begin happening. It's easy for some employees to start thinking about how much time they are putting in, and how little they are comparatively getting paid for all that time. Almost everyone on the team will have those thoughts at some point. That can lead to a wave of exits. People who were with you from the beginning— maybe some of your most talented people—will get tired of pouring in so much without getting enough back. They'll start to think about their other options (and because they're so talented, they absolutely will have other options). In all likelihood you'll go through what I call an exit emergency. This is a painful moment in the life of an entrepreneur. In fact, there are few things more painful in the entrepreneur's trajectory than seeing your comrades walk out the door.

How do you build a company, and a team, that practices *oku* and will hang in there for the climb? The next chapters will cover what you need to know to take your mission to the moon.

CHAPTER FOUR

GET INTO POSITION—F
THE BRAND...

Entrepreneurs grow their businesses one customer at a time—organically. Among the top ten fastest-growing Fortune 500 companies over the past twenty-five years, some 97 percent of their expansion came from organic growth. Starbucks and Home Depot are just two examples.

Once corporations are established members of the Fortune 500, though, they tend to move away from organic growth. How do they grow at that stage? They buy it, through mergers and acquisitions.

If organic growth is the ticket to success, why do entrenched corporations devote so much energy—and so much cash—to M&As? The answer is whispered only in certain Wall Street circles: deal-making beats working. Deals are exciting for occupants of a plush C-suite, while organic growth requires actually running a business. Running anything, of course, is a lot of hard, grubby work. Investment bankers should be talking CEOs out of M&A deals, since a quarter century of data shows that they're not the real road to success. But the huge commissions that accompany high-profile M&As have instead created a cheerleading squad for them.

But for entrepreneurs, truly sustainable growth is best achieved organically. After all, that's where the fun is—becoming financially successful by building momentum for opportunities, customers, and people.

HOLIDAY INN OR DAYS INN? THE DIFFERENCE MATTERS

A key step to growing your business organically is to understand brand positioning.

In the hypergrowth stage, companies try to serve every potential customer. But to reach human scale and position your company to survive for the long term, you've got to decide exactly which market niche is yours and exactly who your customer is.

Let's look at the hotel industry as a way of defining brand positioning. In hotel terms, you're going to have to decide whether you're a Holiday Inn or a Days Inn. Think the difference is moot? Think again.

BRAND POSITIONING: HOSPITALITY

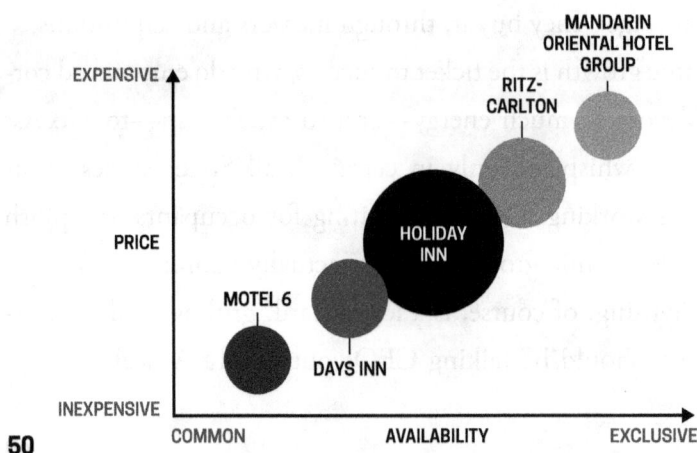

In the brand positioning shown in figure 6, the most common and least-expensive brands are in the lower-left corner, while companies with exclusive products are in the upper right. A sweet spot for entrepreneurs is the upper left: expensive and common (i.e., Starbucks = "affordable luxury").

The size of the circle represents market share and company size. As you can see, Motel 6 has a big, valuable chunk of the market in the lower left-hand corner. This is a company that got its name from the original price of a night's stay: six dollars. Motel 6 is a thriving company that knows who its customers are. There's no fancy cocktail bar in the lobby. There's no newspaper delivered to your room. They'll leave the light on for you, and that's about it.

Motel 6 knows that its niche is the lower left, and it is aligned to serve that part of the market.

Meanwhile, in the upper right is Ritz-Carlton. There, the motto is "Ladies and Gentlemen serving Ladies and Gentlemen." Ritz-Carlton guests expect the staff to know what they want for breakfast. They expect not only a newspaper at their door but the *right* newspaper— no *USA Today* when they want the *New York Times*.

In this quadrant of brand positioning, a business must know the needs and wants of its customers on an intimate basis. It's not only important to know who the customer is, it's important to know who the customer isn't. When you really know your customers, you can create and add value that they find special and that increases the price they're willing to pay. And it doesn't necessarily have to cost you anything extra. Ritz-Carlton discovered that its customers like to be called by their last name; it makes them feel more important—and it makes a $20 hamburger taste better.

Former Ritz-Carlton president Horst Schulze was a mentor of mine. He was a talented leader, but there came a point where his systems skewed out of alignment. For whatever reason, the company could never get a system in place for recording which newspaper each guest wanted. The system they ended up using? Paper and pencil. When customers checked in, the desk clerk recorded their preferred newspaper on a list next to their room number. The company was working to maintain market share in the upper right—but ended up with a system that was more on the Motel 6 level.

Then, Marriott International bought the Ritz-Carlton Hotel Company. Acquisitions impact brand positioning, and entrepreneurs must anticipate how. Ritz-Carlton used to *own* the upper right corner; no one else could take a sizable share of that terrain. But when Marriott International bought the company, the brand's perceived exclusivity suffered, and as a result it fell a notch on the brand positioning chart. That's all it took to make room for the luxury-focused Mandarin Oriental Hotel Group to sweep in and take that valuable market share in the upper right.

Then there's the middle of the chart—the most valuable space of all. The middle of the chart is nearly always occupied by the industry's eight-hundred-pound gorilla. One piece of good news is that the eight-hundred-pound gorilla often gets greedy or complacent—or both—which opens up valuable market share for entrepreneurs to capture. That is where we find the difference between Holiday Inn and Days Inn.

Back in the 1980s, Holiday Inn started chasing Marriott and Ritz-Carlton customers with its launch of Holiday Inn Crowne Plaza. How did that affect the market? In a big way—for Days Inn.

Cecil Day, the founder of Days Inn, noticed something important about Holiday Inn. Despite the chain's great success, Day saw waste in the organization, including 10 percent franchise fees. When Holiday Inn went after the more upscale customer, Day realized that his company could squeeze into the niche just below Holiday Inn.

Day's pursuit of the market was fierce. He wanted to open 365 hotels in a single year: one hotel every day. Where did he get the money for that kind of rapid expansion? He financed each hotel by borrowing against the last one. And how did he determine where to locate each of his new hotels? He built them adjacent to Holiday Inns. Then, he charged travelers 20 percent less. While Holiday Inn was busy trying to pull in the higher-end market, Days Inn became Holiday Inn at a lower rate.

To make the climb from hypergrowth to human scale, and to position your company for sustainable, organic growth, your brand position must be on target. That includes matching your marketing message to your customers' experience.

Too many companies operate like Motel 6 while advertising like they're a Ritz-Carlton. That isn't just a colossal waste of money; it creates big problems. Some years ago, Delta introduced its "On Top of the World" campaign. The ads showed angels fanning passengers as they slept on beds of feathers. In reality, though, Delta had long lines, rigid ticket policies, and awful food—even in first class. Worse yet, it eliminated its legendary Red Coats, the customer service agents who addressed problems. The Delta experience was totally out of alignment with the company's marketing message, and customers punished the airline by fleeing to other carriers such as Southwest, which was fully aligned with its brand. (Southwest didn't even view itself as competing with Delta, but rather with Greyhound, a bus service.)

F*** THE BRAND AND DANCE ON A PONY KEG

When it comes to a brand, don't get so beholden to it that you forget about survival—that's what it's about when you're in fast growth and headed for human scale. Sometimes you've got to f*** the brand to survive. And survive until you get lucky—that's when you get to dance on a pony keg.

That happened to a company I was working with in Jackson, Mississippi. The company was in real crisis mode—it was on the brink of having its credit line frozen and throwing 950 employees out on the street. We had to get face to face with the decision maker and buy time. A call wouldn't do it, so I drove to Jackson to get everybody in the same room.

The bank was ready with numbers to show its case—spreadsheets galore. We know how this movie turns out. Numbers are not usually on our side at this point, so I spoke up and asked if we could get the skunk out of the room. We needed two weeks to find a solution, I told them.

"The company has already had two years to find a solution," the bankers said.

"You've got our full attention now," I said. "Give us two weeks."

"We'll decide later," they said—better than a no.

"Let's go," I said.

The numbers were a mess: expenses too high, receivables too high, inventory too high, and nothing in focus. To find a positive, I bragged about payables—hardly anything over forty-five days. The bank's biggest worry was inventory spoils—items that never sold. The company had more than $2 million in inventory sitting in a warehouse. *What the hell?* I pulled the CEO aside and asked if it could be unloaded at a discount.

"That'll hurt the brand," he said.

F*** the brand—you are trying to survive here.

One phone call later, the spoils had been unloaded to a discount store for thirty cents on the dollar, and every one of those dollars was pledged to the bank.

Still, the bank wouldn't give a hard answer on the freeze, but it did give us the week, which at least covered the next payroll. I was worried, of course, but it's different when it's your ass on the line. I worked with the CEO on a backup plan, which included holding the check from the inventory fire sale until we got clarity on the credit line or using it to make payroll—like swapping hostages.

The next day, a surprised CEO called to ask what I had done. The bank had offered to refinance the credit line and lower the payment to make everything work. "Take it," I told the CEO. I hadn't done anything more to warrant the bank's decision, but two days later, a headline in the news about the bank read: "Sold." My wild guess is that management decided to punt and let the next owner deal with the company.

This firm got lucky. As I said in the introduction, that's how most companies are built. They survive, they get to a boiling point, they hang on, and then luck comes along. That's how Microsoft turned the corner. There was Bill Gates and his room full of programmers not knowing what to do next when luck in the form of IBM walked through the door.

While the Jackson company may never be as big as Microsoft, the recipe is the same for companies large and small. Hang on, even when all seems lost—hang on until luck shows up. When it happened to the company in Jackson, I felt like dancing on a pony keg.

YOUR TURN TO POSITION YOUR BRAND

Here's a simple exercise that can lead to some important, but potentially difficult, conversations about your own brand position.

Bring your management team together and create a brand positioning chart for your market segment. Start by deciding which part of the market is producing your revenue.

Next, where is your competition on the chart, and who are their customers? I always like to know what my competition is doing. And I like to know where they are on the chart, because it shows what we're *really* up against. (The fact that Southwest was competing with Greyhound rather than Delta is enlightening: your competition isn't always who you think it is.) With your competition on the chart, you should start to see gaps.

The next question is the most important: Where *should* you be? Look for the same thing that Day found for his hotels: that valuable slot where you can step in. This step alone may take multiple sessions—and may involve some heated talk.

After you've done this exercise, you'll know who your customers are and where you are in the market. Now it's time to serve those customers and stop wasting your time with the rest of the market.

SAYING NO TO CUSTOMERS— THE WRONG CUSTOMERS

As I mentioned earlier, to reach human scale, you've got to say no to innovation and just start doing. Staying focused on your niche and avoiding shiny objects also applies to customers. You've also got to start saying no to those customers that aren't in your niche. You've got to pivot from "get people to write us checks" to "get *certain customers* to write us checks."

Orvis quickly learned how to say no to the wrong customers—and it has paid off well for the company.

Orvis started out selling top-of-the-line fly-fishing gear and apparel. Then management began to realize that there were some very wealthy people who liked to do outdoorsy stuff—and those customers didn't want a lot of choices. They didn't want to go to Walmart to get their gear. They didn't even want to see inexpensive products next to the high-end products that they were after. They wanted only the premium product, and they wanted it preselected for them. Orvis saw this opportunity and moved into that space; it became the Ritz-Carlton (or, perhaps more accurately, the Mandarin Oriental Hotel Group) of outdoor gear.

You can be sure that Orvis never could have dominated that segment if it was also trying to cater to the big middle of the market.

THE NO. 2 WHO CAN DO—HELPING ENSURE DISRUPTION

Saying no to customers is disruptive thinking—something everyone won't support. That's why one unsung hero is someone I call the "No. 2 Who Can Do."

While the spotlight usually shines on the CEO, the "No. 2 Who Can Do" is a leader who ensures disruption is carried throughout the company during fast growth. Like the head nurse in a war zone, this leader is serious enough to give urgent orders that spur people to action, soft enough to hold a hand in times of pain, and strong enough to show up and do the job day after day.

The No. 2 is usually the smartest person in the room and talks the least, yet gets the most done. Void of ego, this person is happy letting others shine while keeping the company alive and growing.

Titles, offices, and lunches with big-name players mean nothing to a really great No. 2. In fact, all that stuff runs contrary to what a real No. 2 can do.

At STI, Gary Volino was No. 2. He was everywhere in the company, every day. He joined STI when we had forty-eight employees, and he instantly filled two roles: fix problems on the inside, and protect revenues on the outside.

Gary was a five-foot-seven former stand-up comedian and consultant at PricewaterhouseCoopers who had many friends who were CEOs. I once asked him why that was so. "I'm a small-framed guy," he said. "They don't find me intimidating."

He may have been smaller in stature, but his influence was bigger than life. We called him the "Mad Italian" because he worked so hard and was so funny, but in the seven years that he and I worked together, we never had a cross word. In all that time, he also never had an official title. But he was the perfect No. 2, in part because he literally knocked down doors to keep the company going.

One day, I arrived back at the office from New York after beating out some very big players and landing a new account with Ralph Lauren. I strode through the office with a skip in my step and big smile on my face, until I saw Gary hustling down the hall. (That's the NFL of fast growth—not for long is the length of any celebration before the crisis.)

Calm, but concerned, Gary explained that the controller had left the company and locked the payroll checks in the safe, then locked the safe in a storage room with an iron door. We needed to overnight those payroll checks to remote employees, including the new hires at Ralph Lauren. There was no way we were going to start that relationship with, "Our paychecks are late." We had five minutes, Gary said, to get the checks to FedEx.

"Break the safe," I told him.

That was all the Mad Italian needed. He broke down the iron door, broke into the safe, and delivered the checks to FedEx on time.

Breaking down doors—figuratively more than literally—is just one trait of a No. 2. Often using humor, which kept the drama at bay, Gary patched up more things than he ever had to break, including system shortfalls, skill shortcomings, hurt feelings, customer expectations, sales revenue, and strategies for swinging for the fences.

True No. 2s don't necessarily think they should be the second-highest-paid person in the company, but they do want to be significant equity holders—because they truly believe in the company.

When trying to find a No. 2, creating a job description will only build a wall between you and your No. 2, and land you a show horse instead of a workhorse. Often, your No. 2 will emerge from your existing leadership pool. Someone may reach out and say, "I want to work with you." That's because No. 2s are good at finding No. 1s.

CONSULTANTS: A LOVE AFFAIR— AND A TEN-FOOT POLE

In addition to a dynamite No. 2, you will need to add some other crucial members to your team, and you'll also need to shed certain people who are hindering your growth. The next couple of chapters are devoted to these topics.

But first, a word of caution about hiring the people corporations have had a long, slobbering love affair with: management consultants.

As a fast-growth enterprise, do you need a management consultant? The answer: only if the consultant has been in your shoes.

When you need help, you need people who have been where you are, and where you want to go. The vast majority of consultants have never been in your shoes, yet somehow, they purport to know what you should do. No matter what a consultant has done for one of their other clients, they need firsthand knowledge of what you're trying to accomplish—not just what you're trying to sell. The only way to understand what it's like to grow a company from fifty to five hundred employees is to actually have been on that journey.

Instead of looking for a consultant, consider having a mentor. A mentor is someone who's done what you want to do and has no hidden agenda; he or she just wants to help. I've had some great mentors throughout my career who have been available for phone calls and meetings whenever needed. One of them, Tom James, only had one requirement in exchange for his invaluable help: I had to run with him every morning. Believe me, there were plenty of mornings when I thought I would rather pay a consultant than run 6.2 miles before the sun was up. But Tom needed the company, and I needed the help.

Sometimes, though, you need a consultant. However, realize that there's nothing more insulting to employees than a team of consultants who are making the big bucks but have no real loyalty to the company. A consultant fee of $495 an hour works out to a full-time rate of $79,200 per month—or more than $950,000 a year. All for an unspoken agenda that is plainly obvious: the longer they stay, the more money they make. Before hiring a consultant, hammer out an arrangement such as paying a nominal up-front sum for the project, or paying only an hourly rate for on-site talent plus a bonus if they get you where you want to go. In one such arrangement at STI, we reduced the firm's hourly rates from $295 to $35—but they picked up two nice bonus checks.

Unless you've negotiated a fair arrangement, it's best to treat consultants like snakes in a woodpile: only touch them with a ten-foot pole.

Remember: no consultants are worth the time and expense unless they actually help. When STI grew to two hundred employees, we tried to transition the accounting software and had a consulting firm set it up. We then added another one hundred fifty people to the team, which was too much for the software to handle. It began crashing fifteen times a day, but panic didn't set in until it began producing incorrect numbers—then we couldn't balance, bill, or pay.

The CEO of the consulting firm's explanation was, "You don't understand how much stress you are putting on the system. Have you ever heard of an anxiety attack?" I responded, "Yes, I have. You are giving me one. I am living it 24/7." I was advised to hire a larger consulting firm, but they only wanted a long, slobbering love affair.

Finally, I tracked down a controller who had been using the software in a fast-growth company. I hired him and in three days, our system was functional. Three months later, he was a nationally recognized expert on fast growth and on the accounting system. That one-man show was far more valuable to STI than any consulting firm because he was a doer who had been where we wanted to go.

Now, let's look at some more of the key people whom you do—and don't—need on your team.

CHAPTER FIVE

THE HUMAN FACTOR

When building your fast-growth team, there are different types of people and personalities you'll want onboard, and others that you won't.

The biggest hurdle during rapid growth is the human factor—it's the moving, shifting, and replacing of people as the company transitions into the next level of success. It's a challenge because it can be tough to get everyone onboard with the changing mission.

Most high-growth companies start out with two or three founders who share an idea and are passionately committed to a mission, a shared set of values. Work is fun, people work together as a team, and they produce great work. They spend late nights and weekends together to ensure the doors open every Monday morning. At this stage, everyone is important. Everyone has a voice, and decisions are made more often as a team.

That commitment, hard work, and passion toward the mission lead to growth—rocket-fast growth. Maybe the company even doubles in size and revenue. Work is fun and exciting, but always turbulent. All team members have to give it their all to keep the rocket aligned to its orbit, aligned to the mission as it evolves.

Inevitably, however, one of the founders or early superstars won't approve of the new mission, and that's where you get one of the biggest and often most disruptive personalities: the brilliant jerk.

THE BRILLIANT JERK

The brilliant jerk seems like a valued member of the team, but when the chips are down, he or she is anything but a team player.

One of my more memorable encounters with a brilliant jerk happened when I was helping a group of doctors thrash out their shared values as a company.

I spotted him right away. He was the doctor toward the front of the room who, with a few subtle words, was consistently dampening the unity. Every time an idea arose, he had a complaint about why the group couldn't or shouldn't do it. Yet, the entire room grew quiet whenever he spoke, but not because they were excited to hear his input. They listened to him out of respect. That's right—they respected the brilliant jerk.

Why? Because he was so instrumental to the success of the group up to that point. He had been the third doctor to join the group, and he was the highest revenue producer in the room—he brought in twice the revenue of some of the doctors. In fact, without his revenue, the doors of the practice would not be open. Not only that, but he was always the first to step up and cover for doctors who were on call, first to volunteer to work on holidays, and first to get new training—and then share it with others one-on-one. He was also the most published—he had more articles published by the American Medical Association than anyone else in the group.

In short, he had performed brilliantly while the practice was in the venture farm stage. But instead of becoming a contributor to the rocket ship the company had become, he wanted to continue being the brilliant superstar he was during venture farm. He didn't want to step up and take on any new roles and allow any new superstars to emerge.

Brilliant jerks are specialized, high-producing performers, which is what you need in venture farm. But they are not brilliant business-people, which is what you need in fast growth.

My first encounter with a brilliant jerk happened when I was building STI. We hired someone over our heads, someone who had real juice. We marveled at his manic performance. A crisis? No problem, he could solve them all. And his efforts took us all higher, made us all want to perform better. He was worth more than the salary we paid, but he wanted to work with rebels. He believed in our vision and mission. He also knew we couldn't survive without him, at least for a while.

As we grew and added staff and systems and evolved our structure, he began to hold us back. Before long, it was apparent that he was more interested in maintaining his glory than in letting us go and grow. As new stars began to emerge in sales, marketing, and other areas, their light began to shine as bright as the brilliant jerk's high-tech genius. But with the changing dynamic, the brilliant jerk's genius was no longer needed in every meeting. As processes and systems improved, he was no longer the savior in every situation. He could no longer pop into the CEO's office like he could in the past. Before our eyes, the brilliant genius became the brilliant jerk.

Brilliant jerks thrive on the camaraderie of a venture farm, but they struggle to adjust to changing hierarchy and decision-making structures. Without being involved in every huddle, without getting to contribute to every decision, they begin to sour. If the brilliant talent can't learn to let go and let others shine while still contributing to the whole, then they become anchors instead of sails.

So, how do you deal with the brilliant jerk? *Fire him.*

Letting a brilliant jerk hang around is a mistake that many entrepreneurs make. After all, he (or she) made a significant contribution to the company in the beginning, so sheer loyalty compels many entrepreneurs to try to find a way to keep the brilliant jerk on the team. But coddling instead of firing won't change the jerk back into a genius.

Still, coddling is the strategy many entrepreneurs try. They console the brilliant jerk, treat him as special, let him work from home—anything to pacify him. But all that coddling does is kick the can down the road—and keep your company small. You need a team that wants to be led, not managed. Every minute you spend consoling is one minute you should be dealing with customers. After all, they're paying the bills.

Giving in to the whiners takes too much time managing—trust me on this. When STI put 150 additional people on the payroll in one month, it required everyone on the team wanting the next person to succeed. The new class didn't include any brilliant jerks; every person in the room was there to add energy, to make everyone else better.

Over time, brilliant jerks don't add energy. Instead, they suck the life out of the company.

That's what happened at the medical group I mentioned at the beginning of this chapter. The brilliant jerk doctor hung around, unhappy, and kept the company from growing. Then one day, he quit—only to spend the next couple of years attacking the company from every angle. He poached employees, helped competitors, started legal battles.

Now you know why I say get rid of the brilliant jerk.

At STI, I took about eighteen months to get rid of the brilliant jerk because I was so loyal to him. It took that long for me to realize what really mattered: he was putting himself ahead of the brand, and that was undermining our company.

No one should put himself or herself ahead of the brand. While some people say Steve Jobs was a brilliant jerk, by definition, that's not true—he always put the company first.

Once you've fired the brilliant jerk, never rehire him. That's something that at least one CEO learned the hard way.

This CEO's company had grown from $10 million to $20 million in revenue, but the company's brilliant jerk had made the journey a battle with every step. After reading my description of the brilliant jerk in my blog post for the *New York Times*, he and I spoke about his problem. After I confirmed that he, indeed, was dealing with a brilliant jerk, the CEO terminated the employee.

There was, of course, the usual emotionally charged farewell. But that didn't end the CEO's pain. The brilliant jerk pushed back as hard as he could in a vicious fight that included battles in the courtroom and over vendors and employees. No matter what the brilliant jerk threw at the company, I told the CEO: Keep the break clean.

Three weeks later, the brilliant jerk's efforts were beginning to fizzle and it was clear that the CEO and company would win the nasty fight. Then the CEO phoned again with news that I just didn't see coming. "I rehired the brilliant jerk."

I paused for a minute, just to absorb what he said, and then asked, "Why?"

"I think he learned his lesson," he said. "We can turn all this into a positive."

I took a deep breath to keep from blurting out what I was really thinking: *Have you lost your mind?* But I held my tongue because it was a done deal. The brilliant jerk had already been rehired. Everybody had dropped their weapons and hugged.

It was the first time I saw anyone rehire a brilliant jerk, so all I could do was watch and learn. Since the battle had been a daily thing, the CEO had not seen how well his company could operate without the brilliant jerk in the picture. *This will be interesting*, I thought.

During the six-month lovefest that ensued, the brilliant jerk was as brilliant as ever—but without all the jerk. He shined like never before and even told the team that they worked for the best company in the world—he knew because he had looked the world over and could not find a better job or deal.

But after six months, he began to sour. By nine months, the whining was constant again.

When the company moved to a pay plan that included larger commissions on new sales and stopped paying commissions on some old accounts, the brilliant jerk returned in earnest. While the rest of the team was onboard with the idea, seeing it as a fair deal, the brilliant jerk threatened a fight if the old plan did not remain intact. Worse, he tried to poison others to the plan.

In the end, a year after the CEO recognized that he was dealing with a brilliant jerk, he finally fired the person for good. Fortunately, he had the new compensation plan to back him up—since the brilliant jerk did not agree to it, then he was relieved of his duties. At last, the saga was over.

It's not easy to fire a brilliant jerk—someone who has been a top performer. When I let the brilliant jerk go at STI, I was worried how it would impact the team. To my surprise, their reaction was, "What took you so long?" While it felt awful to tell the brilliant jerk he was no longer a match for where the company was going, it felt fantastic the next day—when the rest of the team was able to move forward unimpeded.

Tolerating a brilliant jerk will only bog your company down and keep it from moving up the scale. That's why you must fire a negative member of the team as soon as you realize you have one on your hands.

OTHERS WHO HAVE TO GO

The brilliant jerk is one of the personalities you need to remove when cleaning house to create a high-performance environment. Another type is the duds, the no or low performers. These are the people who can hide in corporate America, but in a start-up, there's no place for them. Duds are those people performing at a level of five or six (or lower) on a scale of ten. They do just enough to get by. They're the ones who are quick to befriend the boss, happy to go to meetings, and first to check game scores or Facebook as soon as they get back from lunch. Duds bring down your company's performance just as much as a brilliant jerk because they put their own interests ahead of the team's and the company's. Keep your duds around long enough and they may even bring the high performers down to their level, or cause them to head for the door. Just like the brilliant jerk, duds have to go.

You've also got to dump the college buddies, brothers-in-law, and other family members who are on the team, but not acting like part of the team. I've gone into plenty of companies that are in the dip between hypergrowth and human scale and more times than I can count, I've found a half dozen brothers-in-law and college buddies all employed full-time as part of the team. What did those guys actually *do* on the team? It's unclear. They just came to help out.

That dip is the time to start trimming the people who aren't doing. Your business doesn't exist to be the employer of record for friends and family. It exists to change the world for your target customer.

In a high-performance environment, team members must earn their spot in the lineup every single day. If brother Bill or sister Sue isn't making the plays day after day, then you've got to find someone who can. Yes, you will make some enemies. You may get dirty looks at family reunions. The next barbecue may be awkward because you fired Uncle Bob. Since close friends and family members can be the hardest to fire, the best policy is to avoid hiring them in the first place. It's that simple.

In the process of tightening up the team, you free up invaluable resources to say yes again and again to your true customer.

HIRING THE HIGH PERFORMERS

Everyone wants happy employees in their workplace. But too often what that means today is what I call "human-resources happy."

In a human-resources happy environment, bosses are at least superficially nice and sometimes pretend to be interested in employees as people. In this environment, birthdays are celebrated, conversations focus on hobbies outside of work, and dogs are welcome in the office. It's basically a lot of HR propaganda that treats employees like children, the idea that being nice to people will get them to work hard for you.

That may work in a second-rate corporate culture where it's more about what people take from the company than what they give for the dollars they earn. But that's no way to build a company—and it's no way to survive hypergrowth.

In the hypergrowth stage, you need what I call "high-performance happy" people. I gave you a taste of what I mean when I talked about hiring high-performing versus high-level leaders in chapter 2. That goes for the rest of the team.

High-performance happy people are more about giving than taking. They bring the skills and a mission-first attitude—the mission is bigger than any single member of the team. They're the Olympic swimmer jumping into the pool at 4:30 a.m. to do laps to earn a place on the team. In a high-performing culture, if one person has a sick child, that's everyone's sick child, so everyone else pitches in a little more that day. That's why high-performance happy builds deeper bonds.

Human-resources happy people, those who are driven by "nice," often struggle in a high-performance happy culture. That's because in high performance, employees aren't driven by "nice." They understand the urgency for growth and are driven—every day—to make it happen. Their happiness comes from being part of a world-class team that is making a difference.

Being nice isn't what built successful companies like Apple and UPS. They didn't waste energy on the phony tactics promoted by standard corporate HR. Instead of bothering with happy talk, they focused on magnifying the outcomes of their high-performing team members.

Steve Jobs was well known for his rants about time clock-punching morons, and yet the high-performing elite at Apple got better, not bitter. Why? Because Jobs focused on Apple's mission—making technology cool. That was more important than a few harsh words or a little immaturity. The results speak for themselves: in 2018, Apple became the first trillion-dollar company in the US.

UPS was another great example of high-performance elite. At UPS, performance reviews were called "agent orange" not only because they were orange in color, but also because they caused intense dread among employees who did not meet or exceed their goals. In the late 1980s, the company was disciplined by the Occupational Safety and Health Administration (OSHA) for its overly harsh, six-week basic-training school for supervisors. Having been through it myself, I can tell you: tough was an understatement. (The program ended shortly after the OSHA complaint.) At the same time, UPS managers were often disciplined for working too many hours, too many weeks in a row. Why did we do it? We truly believed that the US economy depended upon our moving packages from point A to point B.

Employees in a high-performance happy culture are given tremendous responsibility, and they put in the time to show they deserve all that responsibility and more. What makes them happy is not flavor-of-the-month incentives, it is showing the world that they are the best. They don't perform because they want to be liked. They perform because they believe in being great.

Remember these points when building an environment for high performers:

Set up expectations. When hiring high performers to replace your exiting duds, college buddies, and brilliant jerks, let them know up front what to expect, and what's expected of them. Tell them that they should come work for you if they want to work hard and do something truly special. Let them know that if they ask for help, they'll get it, but if they do not ask for help, then they need to be ready to show that they're performing in a blaze of glory and don't need any help, aren't confused, and are completely onboard with what's going on. Also tell them to speak up. Meetings will happen in many formats, from quick huddles to day-long strategy sessions. And when decisions are being made, their input is welcome. But once a decision has been made, they will need to march forward with the team, whether they're happy about the new move or not.

Streamline processes and rules. Unnecessary processes and rules are hurdles for high-performance happy employees. Let them make their own decisions; don't tie their hands with red tape. If you trust them with your mission and with hundreds of important daily choices, you should also be able to trust them to handle their paid time off and the tools they need to get the job done.

Know that "get over it" is natural. Life is not always fair, and neither is a fast-growth, high-performing company. It's not an environment where one side or the other gets its way all the time, nor is it an environment where no one is ever offended. Let your new hires know that there may be some yelling—some directed at them—there may be unequal credit given, there may be blame placed in error. And there may be delayed apologies for wrongdoings. People who stew over imbalance, and can't perform until justice is done, are not going to be a good fit. Instead, it's essential that they learn to not take things personally and, instead, get over it and move on.

Refuse to lay off. Avoid laying off high performers at all costs. As I shared in chapter 3, we were able to avoid layoffs when the company lost 20 percent of its revenue during the 2001 dot-com crash. At that point, we were an Inc. 500 company and in unity to the point that there was near-complete agreement on a pay cut to keep everyone onboard.

That's when I knew we were a high-performance happy company.

WHAT'S GREAT ABOUT GREAT RECESSION GRADS

Pampered. Pragmatic. Persnickety. These are not the employee traits that entrepreneurs are looking for when building a fast-growth company. But those are the traits of many legacy candidates in the post–Great Recession era.

Gen Xers? Gen Ys? Nope. I'm talking about their parents—at least a few I've run across. This group thrived in an economy and work environment that included multiple job offers, signing bonuses, and automatic raises just for showing up. That's a reality that won't repeat itself soon.

Even a decade later, workers have to justify their existence, the value they add, why they are being paid.

The must-have employees stepping up in the new economy are the Great Recession graduates, employees who are entering a new reality in the workplace.

Now, let me be clear: No group is all good, or all bad. But entrepreneurs view employees as either adding profits to the company or taking profits away. Having to justify a salary is an unwelcome idea for employees who remember the good old days.

But postcrisis graduates have learned just that: they need to justify their roles and why they are being paid. They know what it means to be in a fast-growth company where new jobs are being created and every worker must add value. They are hungry to work and have a will to win—those are more important to them than entitlements, praise, and corner offices. They don't question or doubt a job that has a tough mission because they know how to survive, want to make a difference, and will follow a vision.

Many experienced employees whom I interview have lost that drive. They are trapped in the easy-money past and have stopped trying to keep up. One major factor holding them back is their lack of understanding about social media as a business strategy. Experienced employees, I've found, typically have a Facebook account and may be dabbling in Twitter or Instagram. But recent grads use social media to communicate—social media, Google, and online video have destroyed the knowledge gap that used to exist between entry-level and experienced employees.

So, how relevant is experience today? Here's a real-world example. When interviewing for recruiter positions for the MBA entrepreneur program at the Oxford Center for Entrepreneurs, experienced candidates talked enthusiastically about how they would figure out the best places to visit and recruit. But a recent grad would ask, "Isn't all that driving going to take time and money? Why not use the internet instead?" We ended up hiring a twenty-four-year-old with only two years' experience who suggested an integrated social media strategy to motivate hundreds of websites to drive traffic to our site. By the way, the new hire wanted only an opportunity to grow, $45,000 in annual salary, and commission on revenue brought in. The experienced candidates wanted three times the salary and their own offices.

I saw another example in action of how recent grads communicate after hiring five CEO apprentices right out of business school; when not using social media, they preferred challenging each other in an open environment. Within two days, they had congregated in an empty conference room and sat there, face-to-face, collaborating on projects and generating ideas.

Again, I'm not proposing that only new grads are worthy of hiring. I recently hired a fifty-one-year-old legacy employee with a sterling pedigree. In his interview, he didn't dwell on the old days; instead, he approached me with a confident and humble view about a fresh start. He was an experienced employee who "got it." But in my experience, he was the exception more than the rule. Most experienced employees looking to reinvent themselves will be better served doing so for something other than a fast-growth start-up—after all, most start-ups do not have corner offices.

CHAPTER SIX

SALES AND MARKETING— TWO MUST-HAVES ON YOUR TEAM

There's a buzz phrase that's being tossed around to help organizations grow to the next level: "exponential thinking." It's the idea that creative thinking can shift paradigms in an organization. I'm all for that (who isn't?). But exponential thinking is not the missing link in building great companies.

Every true entrepreneur already thinks exponentially—big ideas are the norm. In fact, most entrepreneurs' ideas are much bigger than their wallets or staff. They almost never have the infrastructure to implement even a fraction of what they envision. Just ask David Lee, CEO of United Mobile Solutions, who grew his company from $16 million to $26 million in one year. Where did he go wrong that year? "We tried too many big things. I should have stuck more to the core," he'll tell you.

It's one thing to think exponentially. It's another thing to link your big ideas to the essential infrastructure that you'll need to execute them. That infrastructure includes two essential members of the team: sales and marketing.

THE KILLER SALES SHARK

Unbelievably, a vast majority of MBA programs don't even acknowledge sales, much less teach anything related to it. Most training focuses on different variations of corporate solution sales. But entrepreneurial sales are different. It's about more than just taking orders or filling out RFPs; it's about adding to any order the insight and ideas that your company can offer beyond the initial need or want. It is all about giving the customer a high-value-add solution, collapsing the sales cycle, and "GFC"—getting the freaking check.

As a start-up, growing means finding sales and marketing people who can wheel, deal, and persuade in a fast environment.

A lot of companies don't make it to the next level because the only real salesperson on the team is the founder. It's not the lack of exponential thinking; it's a lack of sales muscle. That's the kiss of death for a start-up. If you, the entrepreneur, are the only salesperson at your company, the only person out there talking about the company, then you're not going to make it.

What you need, for starters, is a killer sales shark.

Before I talk about the traits of the sales shark you need in your fast-growth business, let me first describe the salespeople you *don't* need or want.

When you're recruiting a sales shark, you'll find a lot of would-be salespeople who *appear* to be exactly what you're looking for. But these are people who ultimately won't even bring in enough revenue to justify their salaries, much less launch your product into the strato-sphere. Here are two types that you'll want to avoid:

The Bird of Paradise. Bird of paradise salespeople flaunt their colorful feathers on their résumé, in their interview, and on their first day of work. They generally have a solid relationship with HR, do their busywork very well, and have a smooth approach when working with clients. But *they don't close deals.* Remember: nothing happens in a start-up until you actually *sell* something. So, while birds of paradise will dazzle with pretty sales speak, all they're doing is dancing around the fact that they're just not bringing a lot to the table. If you have one on your team now, get rid of him or her. Better yet, don't hire one in the first place.

The Bellowers. These are the salespeople who bellow about a big deal. They can build bridges with large clients, and they go after sales with big upsides—but they never master how, where, or when to close any deal. Instead, they're always bellowing about what else or who else they need to close the long-lasting deals. Entrepreneurs are often afraid to fire the bellower because they don't want to lose the big contract that's supposedly right around the corner. But in a fast-growth environment, you don't have time to wait for the bellower to land the whale. You need someone who can consistently close.

Like real sharks, true sales sharks move gracefully and efficiently: every motion has the motive to close the deal. They are hungry. They have a high metabolism that thrives on speed. They are financially driven to find sales.

Since sales sharks are predators by nature, they will occasionally have run-ins with other staff, and they will challenge the CFO to give them a commission on any sale that moves. So, you've got to be willing to give—because the sales shark isn't a pest, but rather an efficient hunter who knows how to close a deal and move on to the next one. They're not going to be chummy with every member of the team, but they are ready to work to keep your doors open.

To attract these sales sharks, you're going to need the right compensation plan. Most companies pay salespeople a base salary plus commission, which means month after month the company gives away money for nothing. But as a fast-growth entrepreneur, what you need to offer is a compensation structure with a "nonrecoverable draw"—a guarantee that does not accrue against future commissions or wages.

With the nonrecoverable draw, you give away less money while attracting people who know how to sell. A "draw" is an advance against future commissions, and there are two types: recoverable and nonrecoverable. With both types, the salesperson keeps any commission earned in excess of the draw; that's the incentive pay. With a recoverable draw, salespeople owe the company the difference when they fail to earn commissions equivalent to the draw. With a nonrecoverable draw, they don't have to repay the difference. The nonrecoverable draw attracts great salespeople who know they need time to build a sales pipeline—and who plan to unleash a geyser of sales once they do. In fact, one way to tell the difference between a shark and a bird of paradise is that the bird is more interested in a base salary, not commission-based pay. For true sharks, it's the opposite—their goal is to swim in commissions.

One word of caution: don't make the mistake that nearly every entrepreneur makes—don't promote your sales shark to sales manager. Managing is not the sales shark's strong suit—selling is, and eventually, they will quit to go sell for another company, creating a whole other set of problems.

Frankly, great salespeople don't apply for jobs because they're too busy selling. But they *do* listen to opportunities. But before I talk about how to land your sales shark, let me tell you about another key person you need: a marketing genius.

THE MARKETING GENIUS

The marketing genius is the rarest bird in the KGE talent hunt. While business schools get an "A" in training accountants, they get an "F" in educating marketers. A degreed marketing manager who "manages" a marketing budget is a fixture in big corporations: this is the person who's always talking about branding complexity and who confuses a lot of marketing activity with revenue results. But there is an ocean of difference between a degreed marketing manager and a marketing genius. In fact, the wisdom of KGE says don't bother interviewing degreed marketers because it takes too long to untrain them.

Marketing geniuses, on the other hand, know their chief job is to support sales and move the revenue needle. Selling more stuff to the right customers is the name of their game. They know branding is a residual of revenue, not a precursor to it; they get that branding is emotional and that they have to understand the customers and connect with them to sell more. So, they know how to use branding to pinpoint the most profitable customers, package a solution for them, and increase profits well above the entire marketing budget.

Southern Proper understood that and used it to correct a wrong turn. Founder Emmie Howard built a great business selling apparel for young men ages eighteen to twenty-five. But at one point, she tried to sell to young women the same age. A mistake, but not a fatal one. After recognizing the problem—it was missing its core customers, frat boys—Southern Proper introduced a new line of bow ties that flew off the shelves. That correction by the marketing genius got the company back on track.

Marketing geniuses will gladly accept two types of budgets—zero-based and unlimited. The zero budget is what they get until they show how they're going to raise revenue and profits more than their costs. Once they do that, then they have an unlimited budget. That's the win for them.

There's a point in the life of all companies when everything comes down to marketing. That's something my No. 2 Who Can Do, Gary Volino, and I figured out after years of sweating the small stuff and staying late to clear hurdles around people, problems, and priorities. When that moment arrives for you, you're going to need to know how to recognize your genius. Here are some of the qualities of a marketing genius:

- an introvert who can fake being an extrovert

- prone to thinking out loud, even when alone

- a customer advocate who understands and applies "hidden harmony" marketing—that's when customers know that you're great without you telling them

- a strong understanding of the world of ideas

- a voracious reader and pop-culture fanatic with a keen interest in what's hot, what's gossip, and what's relevant to audiences

- know-how when selling intangibles (that's why sales teams love them)

- persistent and persuasive, not a pushover

- a good storyteller who knows how to grab and hold attention

- a desire to make the world a smarter place

- a strong commitment to innovation

So, how do you find your sales shark and marketing genius? None of the usual places.

FINDING THE NINES AND TENS

The sales shark and marketing genius who will take your business to the next level are, on a scale of one to ten, either a nine or a ten—an eight won't do. Finding these nines and tens is going to take more than wading through a stack of résumés. Instead, consider these tactics:

Identify a single channel to a great pool of talent. Instead of chasing after a single fish, look for a whole school of talent. That's what Bill Gates did. He hired a slew of computer programmers from Boeing. STI did the same with UPS; the first big group of technical superstars came from the shipper.

Always Be Interviewing (ABI). Look at talent acquisition as a constant, never-ending process, what I call ABI. Aim to conduct a minimum number of interviews every week, even when you don't need people. If you hear about someone great, or someone is recommended to you, bring that person in for an interview. And don't let the tens get away. When you find one who wants to work for you, make a place for her or him.

I know this sort of relentless talent acquisition is a stretch when it's a fight to make payroll. When we hired 150 people in a single month at STI, the CFO pleaded, "You can't hire anybody else. You are killing our profitability." I promised that I was through—then the vice president of sales came in. "If I just had one more salesperson, we could kill it," he said. I gave him the green light, but then found myself hiding from the CFO—I scooted into the closest office when I saw him coming down the hall. That's just one example of how tense it can be when you're in hypergrowth and headed for human scale.

Ask your existing nines and tens. Nines and tens hang out with their kind. So, build your team by asking those you have onboard to bring more nines and tens in. At STI, that was Eric—a ten as a programmer. We called him "Billy Jr.," after Bill Gates. Eric was that good.

But we desperately needed another programmer—we needed another Eric. Unable to find one, I asked Eric, "We need another you. Where can we get one?"

"Well," he said, in his quiet way, "I've got this friend, Herb. I'll get him."

The next day when I came into the office, there was Herb. Working. Herb turned out to be a mechanical engineer who had trained at Georgia Tech but was one class shy of his degree. He had all the training, all the brains, but was missing one measly class. And how did Eric know Herb? Through video games. They played together every night. Like Eric, Herb was brilliant. But I never would have found him in a pile of résumés.

This isn't about whether you can attract people with degrees from the finest institutions. I've hired waiters and waitresses who were or became nines and tens. The question is whether your company, vision, team, and work environment can attract the best people. Then you've got to figure out how to keep them.

THE BREAKUP FEE—SKIN IN THE GAME FOR NEW HIRES

What was the hot, contentious issue some years ago that led executives from Apple, Google, Intel, and Adobe to hold secret talks and form a secret pact? It wasn't intellectual property, or AI, or offshore tax shelters. It was talent poaching. Steve Jobs himself was personally involved. He told competitors: "If you hire a single one of these people, that means war."[3]

When employees got wind of what equated to collusion among the employers, they filed a class-action lawsuit, arguing that these actions depressed wages. While the primary purpose of the secret pact seems to have been to retain talent, a direct consequence was that it also likely kept a lid on salaries. The lawsuit charged that the executives' actions were illegal because they prevented employees from earning a better living. The pact violated the same free-market principles that had allowed those companies to demand higher prices and earn higher profits.

As an entrepreneur, I also see the other side. The employees affected weren't exactly poorly paid coal miners exposed to black lung disease. Total annual compensation for the group ranged from $100,000 to $1 million or more. And, speaking from experience, it hurts when you invest time, money, and resources in new hires—only to have them walk out the door for a few more dollars. Not only do you lose your investment in these people, they often take along your intellectual property, business processes, and critical customer information. It can be a hefty and demoralizing loss.

---

3   David Streitfeld, "Engineers Allege Hiring Collusion in Silicon Valley," *The New York Times*, February 28, 2014, https://www.nytimes.com/2014/03/01/technology/engineers-allege-hiring-collusion-in-silicon-valley.html.

So, to keep nines and tens onboard, I developed a tactic I call a "breakup fee" for new hires. Just as a breakup fee may be imposed when one side decides to walk away from a merger, the breakup fee for new hires means they have some skin in the game.

Here's how it worked at STI. We offered talented new staff an ascending salary structure that started low but guaranteed automatic increases each month. These employees started at about 50 percent less than market rate but, by month twelve, they were 20 percent ahead of the market. By the end of the second year, they were 40 percent ahead of the market. By year five, they could be as much as 100 percent ahead of the market—and worth every penny.

With the breakup fee in place, it took us longer to find people who were willing to sign up for what I called the "new deal," but once they came onboard, their hearts and minds were with us. We attracted people with a long-term mentality, and if they did contemplate leaving for other pastures, they knew they had something to lose.

YOU GET A LOT IN RETURN

After you've built your team of nines and tens, you can finally breathe. This is the point where you've finally crossed the "trembling earth," or the worst part of the journey across the swamp. At this point in hypergrowth, you've built some internal infrastructure, but not enough to support even more growth.

Now you're ready to begin investing in LOT: learning, orientation, and training.

LOT is what nearly all successful KGE entrepreneurs make the priority as soon as they have a little cash on hand. (Actually, some lifestyle entrepreneurs use the cash in the bank to go to the Bahamas, buy a boat, or go to Las Vegas. There's nothing wrong with that, but that's not fast-growth entrepreneurship.) Without LOT, you're headed for no man's land: too big to be small, and too small to be big.

Before LOT is implemented, newbies have to more or less figure things out on their own. With everyone essentially making it up as they go, the company is still basically operating with one foot in venture farm. That's wasting time and holding the company back.

Once you invest in LOT, you're finally able to say: *This is the way we do things.*

LOT is designed and implemented by a long-time member of the team who creates curriculum around the company's internal terminology, systems, habits, and structures. At STI, we chose one of our first hires who had worked doggedly for several years but was starting to burn out. With her deep internal knowledge of the company, she was the perfect person to design and conduct our orientation.

Once we implemented LOT, it was a watershed moment. Up to that point, we had been a scrappy operation. But when we started *training people* on our internal operations, we started like a real company. And we weren't small—we had about two hundred people on staff. But the debut of that orientation made us really start to think: *You know what? We just might make it.*

KNOW, GROW, EXIT—FOR EMPLOYEES

There's no question that finding and retaining talent is one of the biggest issues that entrepreneurs wrestle with daily. That's why I came up with a clever—and I think original—strategy for recruiting top entry-level talent at the Oxford Center for Entrepreneurs. The key premise? Hire employees with the intention of increasing their workplace value and landing them a major promotion with another company. I call this Know, Grow, Exit for employees.

Why in the world would any company consider doing this, especially a start-up in hypergrowth? Because everybody in the market is looking for extraordinary talent, people with bright minds and smiles, pleasing personalities, and go-getter attitudes, who never whine or say, "I don't understand."

In a world with big consulting firms like Deloitte and Accenture with their worlds of perks, and tech start-ups and their fields of dreams, how can a fast-growth entrepreneur compete? Having had my butt kicked by these companies, too often landing the runner-up candidate in spite of all the time and expense invested in the search, I found out in a conversation with a Deloitte bigwig that even their top-notch employees usually left after a couple of years.

That's when I came up with the pitch: "Come to the Oxford Center, where you can showcase your talents on a platform that leads hundreds of the fastest-growing companies in America. Not only will they get to see you perform, you will get to learn about these CEOs and trailblazers firsthand." To sweeten the deal, I also tell these A+ millennials that I will coach them on evaluating these companies and basically act as their career adviser. Just like I counsel entrepreneurs before they decide to sell or merge with another company, I'm now an exit adviser for my entry-level employees who are ready to do something else.

This is a radical approach for me because I used to brag about the low turnover rates at STI and push anyone out the door when they decided to leave—no goodbye parties, farewell dinners, or exit interviews with human resources. Nothing. Just a thank-you, and off you go. Under the new strategy, I initially hoped they would hire on and stay. But I was wrong. They still see brighter and greener pastures and leave.

However, they don't take the first offer. They take one down the road after they've done a long due diligence on an assortment of companies and cultures. It still hurts a little, but I am OK with it because it brings in the best and brightest on the front end. Young team members join my company eager to know, grow, and eventually exit. But in the meantime, we have onboard the dynamite talent we need.

CHAPTER SEVEN

LET IT FLOW—SECURE YOUR STREAMS OF COMMERCE

B y 2003, I had built STI into an $80 million company. Depending on your point of view, it was either a tremendous success or a colossal failure. You see, it could have been an $8 *billion* company.

What kept us from getting to that level? Everything that you've read in this book. I made the classic mistakes that most entrepreneurs make. After we had carved out a niche serving Fortune 1000 companies, we got distracted and started chasing a whole other revenue stream. All those wins made us feel like we were on a streak, and we started following shiny objects instead of staying focused on our niche. Those were the years of the dot-com boom, and all those dot-com companies started calling us. "We need you," they said. "We need your product. We want to give you our business."

Instead of sticking with the Fortune 1000—which was rock-solid territory—we were seduced by the fantasy that serving all those new internet companies was the way to even greater dominance.

Companies large and small make some version of this mistake. That fact was on my mind the last time I was in another business that, depending on your perspective, was either a wild success or a serious failure relative to its potential. I was in The Varsity—an Atlanta institution—enjoying my Red Dog (hot dog with ketchup), FO (frosted orange shake), and side of Strings (fries).

What's unique about The Varsity is that it has created its own menu language. That may be one reason what is basically a giant hot dog stand has achieved world renown. Presidents, celebrities, tour buses, and locals like me come in droves for more than a favorite hot dog and sides, we come for the experience. When I go to The Varsity, I get a welcoming sense of familiarity just like I get when I walk into the Empire State Building in New York or Ryman Auditorium in Nashville.

In Atlanta, The Varsity sells a thousand Naked Walking Dogs (hot dog to go on a plain bun) every day of the week. It has expanded to a few locations in the greater metro area—but that's it. Why haven't the owners been able to replicate their success all across the state and the country?

One reason? The same special lingo and atmosphere that helped make The Varsity an icon in Atlanta doesn't work outside that market. At dinnertime, the restaurant is a sea of people elbowing their way through the doors and toward the counter servers who sing out a phrase strung together as if it were a single word: "What'll ya have?" Customers then shout back, asking for favorites like Heavy Weights (hot dog with extra chili), Ring Ones (onion rings), and FOs, among many other custom-named goodies.

The company's satellite locations haven't come close to matching the flagship's iconic status. The last time I visited one of them, about twenty miles from Atlanta, I was almost offended. It had no energy, the "What'll ya have?" was just a whimper, and I'd swear they weren't using the original formula for the FO.

The Varsity was founded as a hot dog stand for Georgia Tech students by a Georgia Tech dropout named Frank Gordy. That was 1928, twelve years before McDonald's was founded. Today, The Varsity is still family owned and has seven locations total. But why hasn't it grown to be at least a regional chain like In-N-Out Burger, which has expanded to more than three hundred locations since its founding in 1948?

Because scaling means much more than just opening new locations. It means replicating both the customer and employee experiences over and over. And you must do that while decreasing some incremental costs as you grow—that's financial scale, the next rung on the fast-growth ladder.

Dave Thomas, founder of Wendy's, understood that. His solution? Keep it simple. That's the golden rule of scale. Dave offered single, double, and triple burgers, and knew that a Frosty was a Frosty, wherever it was offered. Starbucks, meanwhile, built an empire on lingo—tall, grande, venti. But it took thirty years and a lot of work and investment to get there.

Lingo may have built The Varsity in Atlanta, but outside that area, it created an insurmountable hurdle for customers—a layer of complexity to the already death-defying task of scaling. The lingo probably shorted Gordy's heirs stores numbering in the hundreds to tens of thousands.

Building an excellent business is the hardest thing you will do in your entrepreneurial life. You can do it by keeping it simple and scaling it, like Dave Thomas did with Wendy's. Or you can make it great, like The Varsity did. But it's very hard to do both.

Bringing your business to scale involves a dizzying number of variables. And defining success as you scale is subjective. If your goal is three hundred locations, then seven—like The Varsity—is a failure. If you're hoping to clear $1 billion, then the kind of success that we achieved at STI would be a disappointment.

To ensure the success you expect, let's look at how to secure your streams of commerce.

THE RIGHT PRICE

When you're in hypergrowth, you need to price your product mix correctly—and that's hard to do when there's so much noise out there telling you how to choose the right number. Textbooks talk about price "elasticity," posit that you should charge X percent more or less than the incumbent, or tell you to determine the "fair" market value with some arcane calculation. Other so-called experts say that you should calculate 10 or 11 percent over your gross margin, alleging that this is a one-size-fits-all algorithm.

None of these is the way to determine price during hypergrowth. The best approach to pricing is simply to *charge as much as you possibly can*—because you're going to need the income.

Earlier, I talked about going up against the industry's eight-hundred-pound gorilla: IBM. IBM priced its products very high, but we at STI chose to price ourselves even higher. For our niche, we were confident that we had the best game in town, and we underscored this by touting our expertise and setting a premium price. Since IBM failed to prioritize the niche and put its best people on it, we were able to offer a proposition to the Fortune 1000: choose them, or choose us. When we did that with the other Fortune 1000s, more than 80 percent of them ultimately chose us. And it certainly wasn't because we based our prices on an academic formula. We charged as much as we possibly could, and we needed every penny.

In your market, you are the insurgent. You've found a customer who wasn't well served by the incumbent. Remember Mark Segal from chapter 1? He opened a waste-management firm and then discovered that the *instant delivery* of waste-management solutions was the unmet need in the market. His competitors weren't doing it, and that had created headaches for a big swath of the market. When Mark Segal committed to *same-day* solutions, his phone started ringing off the hook.

What does that have to do with pricing? Well, Mark also discovered that he could charge three times as much for an instant dumpster as for a dumpster delivered in two weeks.

The reason you're in hypergrowth, of course, is that you're serving a previously unmet need. Underserved customers are so glad you're in the game that they may be glad to pay a handsome premium over and above the incumbent's price.

Maybe you found your niche by noticing that the incumbent was overcharging. You entered the market to offer a comparable product for less. But notice a pattern here: you're either charging a lot more or a lot less than the incumbent. When your price is about the same as the incumbent's, most customers will just stick with what they know. In both cases, you're charging as much as you possibly can within your particular strategy relative to the incumbent. If you're undercutting the incumbent, you're charging a price that's low enough to set you apart. But don't charge one penny less than you have to in order to achieve that market position.

FIND YOUR GATOR HOLE

Gators live in long, deep holes that they dig along the edges of the swamp. Gator holes are a wonder of nature: they look like they can collapse at any moment, but they are surprisingly sturdy.

In KGE, everybody needs a gator hole—a revenue stream with very high margins. Even if you're already enjoying steady revenue, you should be looking ahead to figure out what you can offer to your existing customers that they will love and that can deliver a higher profit margin than your current offerings.

Starbucks has built what may be the business world's most amazing gator hole. You can order a regular cup of coffee, of course, and you can rev it up with a shot of espresso. But which products does Starbucks push? An array of specialty coffee drinks. And we know how much those cost: for a nickel's worth of steamed milk, Starbucks can charge two or three times what it charges for a cup of coffee. *That's* a gator hole.

Some years after I sold STI, I founded the Oxford Center to offer advisory resources for fast-growth entrepreneurs to help keep them from making some of the expensive mistakes I had made. The Oxford Center's primary revenue came from membership fees, but as we built out our offerings, we found that we could offer members a high-value—and high-margin—product that they couldn't get anywhere else.

We discovered that we could sell their businesses for them. We were the only company offering that service, we already knew them and their business, and we only represented them, not the buyers. We did all of this for a fairly modest membership fee of $2,500. (That also included telling them honestly when they didn't have anything to sell.)

But when they had built a valuable business and were ready to make a cash exit, we were in the perfect position to help. And for that, we might pull in $250,000. Internally, we referred to the service as "the cannon" because all it took was one initial blast to pay all our expenses for a year. But for that, we helped entrepreneurs negotiate the most favorable terms of sale. That made our value proposition to them enormous: they could make millions more, thanks to our help, than if they pursued a sale on their own. So, our high-margin product was also their windfall.

Don't stake your whole future on a revenue stream that's producing 20 percent margins. From your product mix, what can you offer to generate roomy margins? As a rule of thumb, aim for at least 10 percent of your revenue to come from a product with 80 percent margins. That's your gator hole.

CROSS-SELL—IT WORKS

What I just described at the Oxford Center is a form of cross-selling, or bolt-on revenue, which is about anticipating another product that your existing customers need.

Earlier, I talked about how Southern Proper tried to deviate from its young male customer base and offered a line of clothing for young women—and it was a miserable flop. Trying to appeal to new customers is much harder than meeting the needs of the customers you already know, and who already trust you.

Instead, consider the shrewd strategy at your local Walmart. At one point, the megaretailer decided to beef up its garden centers, a calculated step onto Home Depot turf. Customers already come to Walmart for a thousand other essentials, so aiming to meet all of their yard-and-garden needs was a natural bolt-on.

But cross-selling isn't limited to retail. Consider the impressive case of an entrepreneurial doctor, Jeffrey Gallups, founder of the Ear, Nose & Throat Institute. Based in Atlanta, the ENT Institute claims to be the largest ear, nose, and throat practice in the southeastern US. Gallups transformed a traditional practice into an entrepreneurial enterprise that grew so fast that its revenue doubled every eighteen months.

Yet that kind of growth wasn't on his mind when he started his career in 1995. He was a typical solo ENT practitioner when he finished his training. But he had always been a go-getter, working weekends throughout his residency to make additional money. "I doubled my salary doing this," he told me. "I drove a nicer car than my professors. I had momentum even then."

Then his momentum hit a glitch. He was booted from a large, multipractice ENT group for competitive reasons. He was beginning to attract patients away from other doctors in the group, essentially "flipping" his partners' patients into his own practice. "I was gaining on others in the group, and they were very threatened," he said. His is a classic example of how fast-growth entrepreneurs think and work differently.

A boot and rejection can be a huge blow to the ego and pride. "When colleagues come to your office after hours and ask you bluntly to leave an eight-year established practice, it is difficult to see a bright spot," he told me. But a boot can also set the entrepreneur loose—for Gallups, it was the kick-starter, although a painful one, to his current success.

An outcast in the medical community, he went ahead and hung out a shingle and began a solo practice. Having few patients, staff, or doctors interested in joining him stoked his entrepreneurial fire. He needed revenue, so he focused on creating one-stop medical care. In short, he couldn't justify sending patients to another practice for a service he could provide "better and cheaper than the competition," he said. He was cross-selling from day one.

He created ancillary services to maximize revenue per patient, starting with an audiology center. Today, those ancillaries include his own surgery centers, medical labs, and allergy centers.

Over time, he also learned how to squeeze costs out of the system without sacrificing quality of care. For example, he worked with insurance companies on a single co-pay solution for patients who were receiving multiple treatments through his practice.

Still something of an outcast, he was having trouble recruiting enough doctors to work with him. That led him to make a very smart move: instead of trying to convince other doctors to join his team, he asked them what they wanted. Their answer? To practice medicine and not worry about the business side or about managing their retirement plans. Once he knew what they needed, he made it happen; he built an infrastructure that allowed his doctors to see patients 100 percent of the time. He also brought in an expert to develop a customized deferred-compensation retirement plan for all doctors who joined the team. With those measures in place, the eight doctors under his umbrella became eighteen.

Like any entrepreneur, Gallups overreached at one point. The shiny object was a beauty and health spa, which he added above his surgery center because he found a great person to run it. But when that person left, it all fell apart. Ultimately, it was too far afield from his core ENT expertise from the start. He ended up closing the spa after one year.

Gallups's one-stop medical care works, in part, because patients like coming back to a familiar physician and don't like the extra time and expense of seeing a new specialist. Plus, his infrastructure allows him to leverage staff and overhead for several lines of business, helping each line of business operate more efficiently than a stand-alone. That also saves patients money.

Before entering any new line of business to build a revenue stream, ask these questions.

- Can the opportunity produce positive cash flow in less than three months?

- Does it have cross-referral possibilities to other business lines?

- Is it a win, win, win—for customers, the business, and any other essential third party?

- Is it core to the business?

- Does the business have the in-house expertise to at least test it before making a major investment?

SUPPORT GROWTH WITH TCO

As you rocket through hypergrowth, you must also support the revenue streams and growth that you've worked so hard to build by implementing a strategy known as total contact ownership, or TCO. We debuted TCO at STI as a strategy to reinvent IT support.

With TCO, the team member who makes the initial contact with the customer owns the situation from start to finish. Even if he or she is not the person to resolve the problem, the same person owns it until the customer says it is resolved (*not* until the company thinks it is resolved).

For example, if an IT person takes a call that the accounting department needs to resolve, it's that IT person's responsibility to contact accounting, explain the situation, and then connect the two parties. Ideally, that's done with a "warm transfer," in which IT describes the problem to the accounting colleague while the customer listens.

But the responsibility doesn't end there. Follow-up is the most important part of TCO. The problem owner must follow up with the colleague to understand the resolution, and then follow up to ensure the customer is satisfied with the outcome and has no further questions or concerns. Only at that point is the problem deemed resolved.

Moreover, in TCO, the goal is never to pass the problem along to another colleague or department unless absolutely necessary. The goal is always resolution at first contact. And if the problem is merely a symptom of a larger issue—a snag in an internal system or a bug in a line of code—then TCO means having the passion to get to the root of the problem and eliminate it for good.

TCO is also a strategy for reducing costly miscommunication. When a customer describes a problem, the problem owner recaps the issue by restating it in full, and then stating what he or she is going to do about it. This step is critical because about 20 percent of the time the problem is misunderstood or incorrectly heard, or someone else has already attempted to solve it—often using the same solution that the problem owner is about to try. By articulating both problem and forthcoming answer, most miscommunication is eliminated.

The strategy worked so well that STI won an award for excellence in IT support. After that, nearly 90 percent of the Fortune 1000 adopted our TCO standards and best practices for their own IT support operations.

TCO works because it's designed to give customers the three things they really want: timely service, a defect-free product, and care. Customers will occasionally forgive the first two if they think you listen to them and care about their concerns. Otherwise, they turn into heat-seeking, hateful customer missiles.

Ultimately, TCO is simply a name for something more fundamental: how to treat the people who buy your products. It's one thing to say that you'll adopt a philosophy of total contact ownership, and it's a different thing to actually execute it when your entire team has been working twelve-hour days, six to seven days a week, and the phones do not stop ringing.

That kind of chaos will test the mettle of every single team member in a rapid-growth start-up. That's why you need people with traits I described in chapter 2. When we were in the thick of that chaos at STI, the phones were constantly ringing with Fortune 1000 CIOs on the other end of the line. The saying "the customer is always right" is a cliché, but there's a reason it's still widely used: because it's usually true. If they said we did it, we probably did do it. So, we needed to be as nice as we possibly could while we scrambled to solve every problem.

That's what Ashley did.

I can't overstate how lucky we were to add Ashley to our team. Her job was to sit there and answer those endlessly ringing phones—and she had it in her to be kind over and over again. She could answer a call at 5:59 p.m. on Friday as if it were her only call of the day. One evening, when we were wrapping up, she told me she had taken 126 calls that day. She had the determination of those Olympic swimmers jumping into the pool at 4:30 a.m.

And you need an entire team of Ashleys to stay profitable and grow your business to human scale and financial scale. Because the goal, *from the very start*, should be to exit your company.

EXIT

CHAPTER EIGHT

WHEN TO EXIT YOUR BUSINESS

There are typically three types of outcomes when entrepreneurs exit their business. It's a little like watching reruns of good, bad, and ugly TV shows. Unfortunately, the bad and ugly reruns seem more common than the good.

In the good rerun, the entrepreneur is exhilarated with the exit. The market has finally validated the idea at the core of the business and, having proven his or her point, the entrepreneur happily dances across the end zone with a big fat check.

In the bad rerun, the entrepreneur exits in a sigh of relief because it is basically a break-even deal. There's enough money to pay off the bills, and the entrepreneur and most of the team become employees of the new outfit that acquires the company. No trumpets are blowing at the closing table, though. For the entrepreneur—usually an overachiever—an acquisition and a job working for "the man" ultimately are not validation.

The ugly rerun, meanwhile, is painful to watch, and embarrassing for the entrepreneur. This one involves a fire-sale liquidation or a posse of predators—venture capitalists, lawyers, investment bankers, hired executive guns—shamelessly stealing the company out from under the entrepreneur. It's all legal, and all designed to silence the entrepreneur into exile.

The ugly posse takes over a company by using an experienced team of lawyers to get the entrepreneur to sign away his or her life's work through a meticulously orchestrated legal process. Operating with experience and precision, the predators prey on entrepreneurs who know little to nothing about financial shenanigans such as reverse stock splits, down rounds, and stock dilutions. While these terms are yawn inducing, with a stroke of a pen on a legal document, they can reduce a founder's ownership of his or her own company from 99 percent to less than 1 percent.

Here's how it works: the venture capitalists buy minority ownership in the company. Before long, they claim wrongdoing within the company, maybe fraud or even sexual harassment. They take the role of the victim and, under the pretext of verifying the malfeasance, they bring in their buddies as hired guns to do an audit. Their goal? To violate the agreement signed when the posse initially bought the minority stake, turn the founder into a villain, and declare a new CEO from the posse. Before even realizing it, the entrepreneur has exited his or her own company.

Sounds made up? Not so. A silenced entrepreneur who was also a medical doctor and health-care hero came to see me after enlisting "pros" to supply his dream company with cash and coaching. "They treat me like I've exited the company that I started," he told me.

Unfortunately, I had to tell him, "You *have* exited the company. You just don't know it yet."

It was a harsh reality for an entrepreneur who had created the algorithm for diabetes distribution management, worked tirelessly for FDA approval (which carries millions of dollars in intrinsic value), and built an impressive clientele of well-regarded hospitals. These assets made his company the market leader, with hundreds of millions of dollars in enterprise value. He had what most fast-growth entrepreneurs dream of: a twin-flame enterprise that created enormous wealth while drastically improving people's lives—and it had a high-profile board of directors.

But it was a demanding business that required 24/7 management. No algorithm could tell him when to pursue his next growth spurt, and a couple of "doozie" hiring mistakes threw the company off course and disrupted cash flow. He needed outside funds to support the growth strategy and he needed to bring in some professional managers. That's when the "pros" from Wall Street showed up at his door.

They placed a stack of complex paperwork in front of him and, without understanding the full complexity of all the legalese, he signed. What he put his signature to was a series of financial manipulations that included a ten-to-one reverse stock split and two subsequent down rounds. The Wall Street posse was planning to use the doctor as the public face of the company—but had diluted his ownership nearly to zero, and he had been pushed off the board with the direct threat of a lawsuit.

As terrible as a takeover posse is, the entrepreneur isn't an entirely innocent party in such a situation. Entrepreneurs can be so focused on the upside of continued growth that they completely ignore any downsides should a deal go sour. They need cash and crave market validation, so they let the posse in and then are vulnerable to the wining, dining, and jet-setting of the venture capital world. And, of course, signing any document without understanding every word is just asking for trouble—especially when it comes to business dealings for a company built on your sweat and tears.

Entrepreneurs have been getting hosed for years when exiting their companies. Many of them took a long time to know and grow, and then they stumble and fall when it comes to the exit. That's why the *exit* may very well be the most important part of KGE.

In the final chapters of this book, I'll talk about the hazards of the ugly exit—to prepare you for landing the good exit that you've worked so hard for. I'll also talk about how to reset the rules of the exit process to favor the entrepreneur.

WHEN GREAT BUSINESSES GO OUT OF BUSINESS

We know that the vast majority of businesses fail; that's old news. Oftentimes, the reason for a company's failure is pretty clear—few tears are shed over the failure of a company that sells a product no one wants.

But it's startling when a business that appears to be a roaring success shutters. Loyal customers are left confused and wondering: "What went wrong? How did such a great business fail?"

That's how I felt when I first heard that the legendary Harold's Barbecue in South Atlanta was closing for good. The eatery had been an institution since 1947, with a long line of customers winding around the building almost from day one. To get to the bottom of the matter, I called Harold's. Linda, my waitress for years, answered the phone. "Harold's," she hollered.

"Are y'all closing?" I asked.

"When we're done Friday, we ain't coming back," she said, and hung up the phone.

What initially seemed like a bad rumor turned out to be just a run-of-the-mill bad exit. And Linda's answer perfectly defined what that means: the business locks the doors and everyone leaves for the last time. No big check to take to the bank. No end-zone victory dance. No job to go to tomorrow. For employees and customers, the bad exit can be more devastating than a bankruptcy, because nobody sees it coming.

Too often, bad exits hit businesses that could have been passed on to a new generation, or even become a regional enterprise with multiple locations, but a sudden departure of the founder or leader derails them.

With Harold's, the founder and namesake had passed away a year or so prior to the restaurant's closure. But even when he was at the helm, the way he ran the place had all the makings of a bad exit—in spite of the fact that he made epic barbecue.

For starters, Harold collected every penny at the cash register. That meant there was never a system of checks and balances for openings and closings. Also, he didn't have an inventory system. That left the business wide open when Harold passed away. Since Harold had done it all himself, nobody else knew what to do or whom to trust. Any business wanting to avoid a bad exit must be able to routinely open and close without the owner being on hand—that includes not being available by phone, email, or text.

Harold was also the only member of the team who knew how to turn the meat—the most important asset for a barbecue restaurant. The exceptional flavor of Harold's meat, which was slow cooked at a low temperature, made up for the mediocre customer service, high-priced platters, and worst location imaginable—right next to a maximum-security federal penitentiary. He had, apparently, never even considered the value of that perfect meat recipe because he never bothered to share it with anyone else.

Harold's considerable vulnerabilities left the restaurant unable to sustain itself in his absence.

While Harold's story may not seem as tragic as the doctor entrepreneur who was bamboozled out of his own company, both of these exits are devastating for children, other heirs, employees, and customers. Surprisingly, both exit scenarios are all too common—and entirely preventable. Harold's is all about aligning internal systems. But even when that's done, you've still got one hell of a fight ahead of you. Winning that fight starts with a commitment to selling the future.

EXPLAIN THE PAST, SELL THE FUTURE

From the moment an entrepreneur has an idea for a company, all the way through the venture farm, hypergrowth, human scale, and financial scale phases, the entrepreneur must keep in mind what's most important during the exit—to get the maximum purchase price for the company.

Up-front cash and guarantees should be the driving principles for the entrepreneur—because on the other side of the table, buyers will strive to pay the minimum price for the company while deferring payments and not guaranteeing them. While these are polar opposite objectives, the exit really does not have to be a fight between the buyer and seller. It is all about the entrepreneur framing a market reality that prevails, and that the buyer pays for, instead of the normal exit carousel of lawyers, accountants, and investment bankers using a methodology that ultimately works against the entrepreneur.

KGE is about resetting the playing field, rewriting the exit rules from the time before the doors open until the day the entrepreneur walks away with a big fat check.

To do that, the entrepreneur must understand three players during the exit that can tilt the rules against him or her: investment bankers, attorneys, and accountants.

The first of these is the investment banker. In truth, these players are little more than glorified real estate agents. Since they have to justify their tremendous fees, they bring in grunts (recent MBA graduates) to work one hundred hours a week turning out hundreds of pages of impenetrable analysis. After all the hours, late nights, and fancy number-crunching, investment bankers typically end up proposing a sale price based on a market comparable—just like real estate agents do when they find another house that sold on your street. For their role as the facilitator of the sales process—basically the player who handles the paperwork—the investment banker should have a value of around 1 percent of the sales price, with a cap of $100,000.

The next players in the exit game are the attorneys. To level the playing field, the entrepreneur must tell all attorneys involved that they are *not* running the deal. Instead, they are in charge of drawing up documents and giving counsel when asked—or when they see a mistake is being made. Otherwise, the attorneys will try to run the deal according to their own rules while racking up scores of billable hours at obscene rates.

Accountants play a pretty straightforward role in the exit process. They sign off on the company's financial reports as being "true representations" of the company's performance. However, do not let the accountants help in what should be the first step in the exit process: explain the past, and sell the future.

That is how you come up with a new market comparable—a higher price—so you're not pigeonholed into the last deal made. To get the maximum price for your company, you must use financial data to show where you've been, and then make the case for where the company is headed. For example, if you've opened ten stores, that's the past. It's the next one hundred stores that will increase gross margins and double your profits. KGE explains the past but then frames the sale negotiation around the future.

No matter how good or bad the past, the new market value is the future. You must *sell* the future by capturing the excitement and potential of your company's growth.

How does this work in practice? Well, investment bankers and buyers will typically propose a valuation that's around five times EBITDA (earnings before interest, taxes, depreciation, and amortization). But EBITDA is the wrong yardstick for valuing a company—and you're going to show them why.

BASE SALE PRICE ON GROSS REVENUE, NOT EBITDA

With a sale price based on EBITDA, you're not so much selling your company as you are handing over control of it to a buyer who will use your own profits to pay you back. Worse still, the EBITDA calculation is not an objective, rock-solid calculation. Calculating EBITDA requires a series of judgment calls that ultimately produces a subjective result. By allowing that subjective number to serve as the basis of the sale price, you give the other side a hundred different ways to pick you apart in the due diligence that precedes a sale—all designed to lower the price of your business. Due diligence actually happens at the end of negotiations, when it's easier to wear down an entrepreneur who's tired of the process and ready to accept any deal—even a bad one.

Solve this problem by insisting on gross revenue (your total sales), rather than EBITDA, as the basis for calculating the sale price. While EBITDA is subjective and allows the other side to poke holes in the deal, gross revenue is a solid base point. It starts clean and will stay clean throughout the sale process. If the other side claims that the business is worth only $20 million even though it's at $40 million revenue, then they're saying it's worth 0.5 times gross revenue. Whatever the offer on the table, insist on expressing it in terms of gross revenue.

As part of selling the future, you must make your case for why your company is the greatest—until you really are. Back up your statement of greatness by describing the new standards you are creating and how those standards will reshape your industry for years to come. Google and eBay had hundreds of competitors on the web when they started, but they both set new standards for the industry. Find and frame any of the points in the McKinsey 7S Framework that make up a new market comparable, and the more the merrier: you are an innovator, you scale your enterprise with repeatable practices, your team is loaded with super talents who produce every day, you are extraordinarily easy to do business with. That is the KGE way of declaring leadership. For inspiration, I like to think of Mark Zuckerberg and Muhammad Ali, two great entrepreneurs who each set the example for his field. They stated they were the greatest before they were—and then they made it come true.

A while back, my team at the Oxford Center helped a marketing services business sell itself to a much larger company. The buyer originally offered the standard five times EBITDA. But we didn't accept that valuation. We went on to frame the negotiation not simply around the company's prior fast growth, but also on what its trajectory promised for the future. And we insisted on using gross revenue as the basis of the company's valuation. How did that shake out for the final sale price? The number we settled on was the equivalent of *thirteen* times EBITDA.

Again, the exit doesn't need to be a fight between the buyer and seller. It's not about fear, power, or position. It's about whose market reality will prevail, which is sometimes known as horse trading. Before I negotiate as an entrepreneur, I have to know two things: the kind of horses the other side wants and the amount I'm willing to give up my horses for.

IRREFUTABLE NEGOTIATING TACTICS TO "GET MORE FOR YOUR HORSES"

I learned how to create a market reality from my dad—when I was all of nine years old. In the middle of a recession, my dad decided to buy and sell horses to bring in extra money. Dad's market reality was that he could only afford to shell out $200 to buy a horse, and he had to buy one worth more than $200 to make any money on his deals.

The morning of his first horse trade, my dad dressed in old overalls and worn-out boots—seriously, he had to wrap wire around the boots to keep the soles on. I rode with him out to meet the seller, who was asking $500 for his horse. Dad decided to frame the negotiation around money: he told the seller he only had $200 to buy the horse, and that the bank would not lend him any additional money. The way he was dressed, he looked the part. He also told the seller that it could take him a year or more to sell the horse for $400 or $500. In that time, he pointed out, the horse could get sick or easily eat at least $500 worth of feed—netting the seller zero.

Dad's tactics worked. Everyone was shocked when he came home with the horse—after paying just $200 to a seller who'd been asking $500.

We kept the horse for about a month, and then dad decided it was time to sell it. He put an ad in the local newspaper advertising the horse for a sale price of $1,000. We all thought there was no way he was going to get $1,000 for a horse he had bought only one month earlier for $200. No one could understand his logic.

But dad wasn't *trying* to be logical. That would have meant trying to double his money by selling the horse for $400. Instead, dad was negotiating, and as the key part of that negotiation, he was setting a new market reality. When potential buyers came to look at the horse, dad reinforced that new reality with a new look. He was clean shaven and wore a cowboy shirt, fancy chaps over his jeans, and new boots with spurs. He looked like the Marlboro Man—someone who could easily own a horse and sell it for $1,000.

As he negotiated a price, my dad really showed off the horse's assets. He had it cut and prance, and he showed how it could walk backward and had a nice gallop. The interested buyers, a young couple, had brought their son with them, and they all fell in love with the horse and the idea of the cowboy way of life. They weren't just buying a horse; they were buying a lifestyle: the American West.

That couple bought the horse that day, and they gladly paid $1,000—the full asking price. Dad had used positive reinforcement as his strategy to support his market reality, both as a buyer and then as a seller, one short month later.

The buyers were happy. Dad was happy. And the rest of us were amazed.

Dad's approach underscores what I mean when I say you must create a new market reality for your exit. In market reality, my dad helped someone sell a horse, and he helped someone buy a horse. "Show me the money" may have become an iconic phrase thanks to its use in the movie *Jerry Maguire*, but it's not how entrepreneurs create companies. Instead, there's another line from that movie, spoken by Tom Cruise's character, that is more likely to help you win in a negotiation: "Help me, help you."

That's what creating market reality on the other side is about. And to do that, you must understand these powerful negotiating tactics:

Embrace the other party's agenda. Find out and then understand the point of view of the person you will be negotiating with. To do that, ask yourself these questions: What represents a successful result for the person across the table? What will constitute a win for them? How can I make them look good?

You don't get to enjoy a victory lap in negotiations until you have walked a mile in the other person's shoes. The couple who bought that horse from my dad were thrilled because he sold them the future they wanted.

Represent the market reality you are asking for. Sam Walton drove a Ford F-150 pickup truck because he wanted to look like a low-cost seller. Even when he was a billionaire, he kept driving that truck. It would have been hard to convince his suppliers to squeeze their margins if he'd pulled up in a Maserati. My dad must have understood that strategy, because he used it—with his attire—when buying and then selling his horse.

As I shared in chapter 2, I employed that strategy myself when STI was in its early days—I figured out that I couldn't drive a Bronco and sell to Fortune 500 executives. I had to look the part, and so do you. You need to be who you say you are 24/7, not just during work hours. If you are selling yachts, you'd better walk that walk.

Know whether time is working for or against you. During the Vietnam War, the Viet Cong government knew Americans could not stomach watching the tragedies of war on television, so its strategy was to outlast negotiations. When Secretary of State Henry Kissinger tried to get right to the issue of ending the war, the Viet Cong leaders burned time by holding talks about *where everyone would sit*—before the actual negotiation could even begin.

In most cases time will not be on your side. Investment bankers and lawyers will do everything they can to extend the time. That's how they eventually get the price down while also pushing the billable hours up. At the Oxford Center—where negotiations for more than a dozen different sales on behalf of members may be taking place at any point in time—we put a time limit on the term sheet. That term sheet states the intent to sell but gives a limit of thirty days to sign the letter of intent. That's nontraditional, to say the least, but it's an effective way of resetting the playing field in favor of the entrepreneur.

Never split the difference. The idea that you should get to a final valuation by "splitting the difference" between the buyer's offer and your asking price is a lot of bull. That approach could only work in a world where both sides have in good faith stated a "fair" price. That's not the world we live in.

Splitting the difference is lazy negotiation, pure and simple. Remember, the process of negotiating a sale is about whose market reality will prevail. Rather than splitting the difference with a counterpart who may or may not be negotiating in good faith, stay focused on ensuring that it's *your* reality that comes out on top.

Sell your story, not your values. The winner is usually the person with the best story. Abraham Lincoln was a lawyer, but he ran for president on the story of his earliest years, how he was born in a log cabin and learned to split wood. Stories sell. Values, on the other hand, don't necessarily sell—because other people may legitimately have values that are different from your own.

At one point I was in a negotiation on behalf of Chick-fil-A, a company that had a very clear articulation of its internally shared values. The team's vision was to "glorify God in all we do." In other words, the company's french fries, buildings, and work were all supposed to be a reflection of God. That message wasn't in the marketing to the general public. Externally, Chick-fil-A ran billboards that were fun and upbeat, with cows writing cute messages. Then what happened? The CEO made a public, derogatory comment about gay marriage, and the company found itself in PR hell.

Don't assume that values will sell. They may even sink you.

Instead, sell your story, and make it a good one. What *is* your story? Write it down. Make a video about it. Then use it to reinforce your market reality.

It's not about what's fair. Don't allow business negotiations to turn on personal circumstances. You get what you negotiate for. And those negotiations should be based on market reality.

When you're going to lose, don't go for broke. Instead, get creative. When the deal is about to fall through, don't "go for broke." Don't issue an ultimatum. Don't present a final "take it or leave it" offer. If you're going to lose, it's time to come up with something very creative—something that isn't even on the table. How can you create new value without a lot of additional cost? Maybe the seller stays on as a consultant for a specified period. Or maybe the seller carves out one little division to keep, and then sells the rest. What can you do to make the overall sale more attractive?

Be specific about the past and realistic about the future. Your company's past is already memorialized in numbers and facts. Don't try to revise that reality. As a negotiating tactic, explaining the past while selling the future means discussing past issues so that all parties understand them. For example, "Gross margins declined because we invested in IT infrastructure." Then be realistic about what that past means to the company's future. "We will now be able to scale and franchise one hundred stores over the next year." *That's* selling the future.

Deal with deadlock. Impasses will occur in just about any negotiation process. To deal with it, take a step back, even if it's just for an hour or two. That might involve shifting to a new setting and changing the context of the negotiation. I sometimes go see a movie, or read an entire newspaper.

Then, it's time to turn on your high EQ, or "emotional" IQ. Look for a way to disarm the other side. When he hit a deadlock in a hostage negotiation, and the demands reached unreasonable levels, famous negotiator Chris Voss would ask nicely, "How am I supposed to do that?" That can be enough to turn the entire negotiation around.

In KGE, rather than go for broke, get creative—and, in deadlock, get innovative. A deadlock is actually a healthy part of the process. After taking a break from the action, reset the table. Add new agenda items, with other benefits and features. If you're a smart negotiator you can come back from a deadlock with momentum.

Make the first offer. The old thinking is to let the other side go first. That's wrong. Instead, make the first offer to frame the debate and set the parameters of your market reality.

Understand the people, not just their positions. It's not about your counterpart's stance in this particular deal. It's about who they are. Consider their background, their habits, their strong and weak points. This will allow you to see past their stated position and then bring additional value to the negotiation—by proposing something interesting to them that was never on the table.

Disarm the opposition. Humor and sincerity are the best tonics to dilute animosity and opposition. Look for ways to make a connection with your counterpart about their children or favorite hobby. Football? Boating? Anything that takes the steam out of the room and disarms them.

I like to make a little joke about my education from West Georgia College. Since buyers probably have done their homework on me, and therefore likely know that I started an MBA program at Emory, they might come into the room feeling a little defensive. But negotiators are often Ivy League graduates, so mentioning that I went to West Georgia is a little disarming—maybe they think I'm saying they're smarter.

When things turn personal, head back to strictly business. Negotiations are tough—they can get emotional and personal. It's natural for the other person to try to save money or get his or her way. Remember that before you sit down to negotiate. When things start to get personal, bring it back to the business at hand.

The truth about sandbagging. All sides sandbag. Even when people say they've given the deal a lot of thought and this is their best offer, there's *always* wiggle room; there's always a degree of sandbagging in what they've put on the table. This happens internally, too. Every year, I used to ask my senior leaders to set their metric goals for the next year, and I'd tell them they would be evaluated on that basis. When they gave me their numbers, I knew full well they were holding back a little, and I'd go back to them and give them a nudge to say, "Let's stop the sandbagging."

The truth is that we don't feel satisfied in a negotiation unless we've gone through a process of bargaining back and forth. There's something about that process that provides a sense of achievement. We all like to feel like we've won something—we want to feel like the time we spent was justified.

Negotiations are not search-and-destroy missions. One of the few sure things I know about business is that if you have your foot on someone else's neck, at some point in the future, you can expect to have that person's foot on *your* neck.

In the exit negotiation, we're seeking a win-win. Look at the big picture, including your long-term interests and the relationships hanging in the balance, and you'll see that this negotiation is bigger than the current stakes.

Let me use Sam Walton as an example yet again—but this time, of what *not* to do. Walton used to annihilate small companies. He'd set prices so low that they put his suppliers out of business, and then they'd read the fine print of their contract and discover that, in the event of them shutting down, Walmart had claim to their intellectual property. *That's* a search-and-destroy mission. (As a matter of fact, my own company's negotiation with Walmart was one of the few instances where I actually got up and walked away from a customer. I simply did not want to continue doing business with the organization.) For Walmart, those chickens have come home to roost. Walton himself was gifted enough to pull off such shenanigans, but when he left the company, other folks couldn't do it. I would argue that Walmart has lost out ever since by failing to score deals with some of the best companies.

Even if you "win," don't simply clear the table and walk away. Give the appearance that you're rooting for their success. It's not about sinking the other side. Make it a positive loss and an earned opportunity ahead. Never treat any single negotiation as if it were the end of the road.

The art of closing a deal is staying focused to the very end. Think you've won? Not so fast. The details are where the deal really gets decided. Often, the deal is truly decided at the end, when most of the parties have gone home. And this may actually be the rare place where the small company has the advantage over the big company. For the people at the big company, what's at stake isn't so personal. If your counterparts are concerned with what time the last flight leaves, take their absence as an opportunity to steer the final outcome. Don't be the one who runs off to the golf course or catches the next plane out. Instead, be the person who sticks around and squeezes the most value out of those final details.

The tactics I've just laid out here require mental discipline. That means your work will need to start even before the negotiation begins, with thorough preparation. I go through each of these tactics before every single negotiation, and then I write out a script. That gets me focused and disciplined. Then, once the negotiation has commenced, I'm tuned in to anything that veers off course, and I can correct it quickly.

You've got to be ready for whatever the other side brings—even if they sweep in like they're your new best friend or family member.

That's what happened to an entrepreneur who sold his highly successful wholesale horticultural company. Through hard work, new processes, and patented technology, he had mastered the growth of a particular plant and was selling it to greenhouses all over the world. When the company reached $14 million in revenue, it attracted the attention of a $500 million corporation. The corporation's CEO flew in on a corporate jet and said he did not want to *buy* the smaller company—instead, he wanted to "welcome" it into his "family." He then flew the entrepreneur to his corporate offices, where everyone told him how excited they were to welcome him.

When the entrepreneur got home and finally received the letter of intent, it sure didn't read like a welcome-to-the-family message. It was a bid at a takeover in hopes that a gullible entrepreneur would simply sign on the dotted line.

Don't let yourself be taken in. If you follow my proven tactics for negotiation, you can get what you deserve for your business, have a lot of fun helping the other side help you, and build bridges (not burn them) for any future rounds of negotiations.

DON'T LET EGO GET IN THE WAY

Ego can be the entrepreneur's downfall. That's why letting go of the ego is critical to a successful exit.

Entrepreneurs often let their egos and their need for validation cloud their judgment in the exit process. That's often what leads them to accept a seemingly attractive offer with unfair terms—and then they get screwed. Instead of seeking validation from the market, remember that you have the KGE playbook on your side. You have the tools to reset the playing field and walk away with the best possible deal. But that means setting aside your ego.

Emotions can also get in the way during negotiations. As an example of what *not* to do when emotions run high, look at what happened to the owners of California Chrome, winner of the Preakness and Kentucky Derby horse races.

With a champion's heart, meager investment, and a modest pedigree, California Chrome was, in my book, the very personification of the entrepreneurial spirit. Then the owner ran him in the Belmont Stakes in pursuit of a Triple Crown—and blew it in the most public way.

While other billionaires and corporate owners shell out millions trying find a champion horse, California Chrome's co-owner, Steve Coburn, spent a fraction of the money on a chestnut colt that was a lesser horse on paper but had the fire in the belly to win on race day. That's entrepreneurship: being an opportunist and finding a way to win in spite of having few, if any, resources.

But Coburn apparently didn't understand that you don't *always* win. After his two big wins—at the Preakness and Kentucky Derby—he wasn't ready for defeat and despair. In other words, when California Chrome came in fourth at the Belmont, Coburn fell off his high horse and hit the ground hard. Welcome to entrepreneurship.

In his low emotional state, Coburn lashed out, accusing the winner of taking a "coward's way out." While California Chrome had run three races in five weeks, he pointed out, the winning horse hadn't run in the Kentucky Derby and therefore had "fresh legs."

Coburn's mistake, of course, was saying anything other than "congratulations." As an entrepreneur, when you lose, the way to save face for yourself and your team is just to bite your tongue and shut up. Save your energy for the next competition, which may be just around the corner. Entrepreneurs should never make big decisions or announcements after a big loss (or a big win, either). We'll blow it every time because of all of the emotion (and ego) involved.

Coburn apologized later, but it was too late. He had already disgraced himself and his team. As my grandmother would have said: "Whatever is in the bottom of the well comes out sooner or later." If the right stuff always comes out of your well, then you won't find yourself losing face and having to apologize later.

MANAGE THE TIMELINE

Time kills deals. In the KGE exit, we don't have time for lawyers and accountants to string out the sale by days, weeks, and months for the purpose of increasing their billable hours while putting the deal in jeopardy. KGE shortens the exit time line to a fixed number of days, and holds everyone to that time line.

A mergers and acquisitions attorney once told me that, of all the exit deals that reach his desk, 70 percent are never completed. They either blow up over frustration on one side, or they wither away because no one can craft a final agreement. To avoid that fate and keep everyone on track, KGE sets strict time limits as you will see in the following comparison of the old model of exit strategies and the model of the KGE exit.

EXIT PROCESS: INVESTMENT BANKING
BUYER TILTED. COMPLEX / LENGTHY PROCESS WITH LARGE MONTHLY AND SUCCESS FEES.

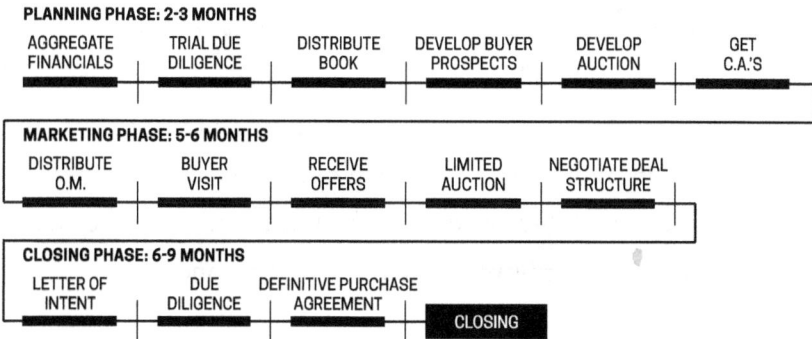

PLANNING PHASE: 2-3 MONTHS

| AGGREGATE FINANCIALS | TRIAL DUE DILIGENCE | DISTRIBUTE BOOK | DEVELOP BUYER PROSPECTS | DEVELOP AUCTION | GET C.A.'S |

MARKETING PHASE: 5-6 MONTHS

| DISTRIBUTE O.M. | BUYER VISIT | RECEIVE OFFERS | LIMITED AUCTION | NEGOTIATE DEAL STRUCTURE |

CLOSING PHASE: 6-9 MONTHS

| LETTER OF INTENT | DUE DILIGENCE | DEFINITIVE PURCHASE AGREEMENT | CLOSING |

EXIT STRATEGY: ENTREPRENEURS
ENTREPRENEUR/BUYER BALANCED. SIMPLE, EFFICIENT, WITH PROPER SAFEGUARDS AND MAXIMIZED NET WORTH

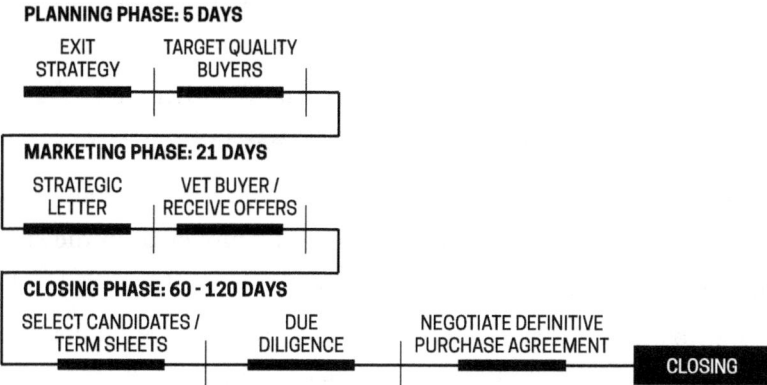

PLANNING PHASE: 5 DAYS

| EXIT STRATEGY | TARGET QUALITY BUYERS |

MARKETING PHASE: 21 DAYS

| STRATEGIC LETTER | VET BUYER / RECEIVE OFFERS |

CLOSING PHASE: 60 - 120 DAYS

| SELECT CANDIDATES / TERM SHEETS | DUE DILIGENCE | NEGOTIATE DEFINITIVE PURCHASE AGREEMENT | CLOSING |

Figure 7: Stay or sell?

As you see in figure 7, the KGE exit allots less than a month for targeting buyers and marketing the sale, and then limits the closing phase to sixty or at most 120 days. Impose this time frame by clearly stating, and then enforcing, a thirty-day time limit on letters of intent and a ninety-day time limit on definitive agreements. Not only does this help get the deal done, but it actually increases the price the entrepreneur ultimately gets—because more time gives the acquisition posse more time to pick the price apart. The shorter process also results in less overall work, both in terms of back-and-forth and paperwork, and less money paid to lawyers and accountants.

Of course, keeping to this timeline will require some muscle. When I was selling my company, STI, in 2003—before I had codified the principles of KGE—we had been negotiating for more than six *months*, and we still had nearly eighty unresolved issues. I decided I needed to call a time-out. I told everyone to get in one room and resolve the outstanding issues—or else call off the deal. Lawyers on both sides screamed, but we did it. The buyer and I led the charge and we resolved seventy-two of the issues on that one day.

REPS AND WARRANTIES

Reps and warranties are the rattlesnakes in the woodpile for exiting entrepreneurs.

Reps are legal and binding representations that the seller and employees make about the company's current and past status. These reps are often loosely stated in the contract but, since they are legally binding, they can trigger clawbacks to extract money from the entrepreneur after the sale. If the buyer goes to lunch with your head of sales, who projects that your company will grow 50 percent next year, that is a representation that can come back to bite you.

Warranties pertain to the future performance of the company and are intended to protect the buyer in the event of weak performance.

Reps and warranties are the "gotchas" that live long after the sale has closed. Of all the traditional rules of the exit process, reps and warranties are the ones tilted most heavily against the entrepreneur.

Investment bankers downplay the significance of these clauses, which can sometimes add to the entrepreneur's tendency to underestimate the power of what are umbrellas of liability.

Consider the case of one entrepreneur who sold his high-tech company to a private equity group. After the sale was complete, the private equity team took some big risks and screwed up the company. We were surprised they were taking such risks—until we discovered that the entrepreneur had signed an open-ended reps and warranties clause that left him *responsible for future profits*. The deal also specified that half of the sale price would be put in escrow and released only on the basis of future performance. After the private equity group ran the company into the ground, investors reclaimed the money in escrow—and then sued the entrepreneur for the other half of the sale price, which they were able to do thanks to a clawback clause that was also in the contract.

In a KGE sale, the entrepreneur gives the buyer all the necessary information about the company's status. Then we require a buy-as-is clause that protects the entrepreneur after the sale has closed. If the other side insists on reps and warranties, the most you should offer is a one-page list of specific types of warranties that are verifiable facts about the company's track record. That's it.

HOW TO DEAL WITH LOWBALL OFFERS

Lowball or "submarine" offers are part of real-world negotiations. If someone throws you a lowball offer, don't view it as an insult. Don't simply reject it. Look at it as an interested customer. Respond by explaining the past but selling the future, and explain why you see it as the market reality. This can be surprisingly effective. It shows that you respect the other side.

Consider how one lowball offer in a real estate sale was viewed by both sides as a productive starting point. When the buyer submitted his lowball offer to purchase the property, he did so in a very thoughtful manner. In a letter that accompanied the offer, he explained that he had used data from the Case-Shiller US National Home Price Index and from the National Association of Realtors to come up with the price he offered. "It will be tempting to view my low bid as an insult," he wrote. "Please don't make that mistake. Your home is genuinely appealing, and I wouldn't have written this note unless I was serious about buying it. Getting a firm offer in this market is an accomplishment. So, congratulations!"

The seller responded in a very reasonable way. In reply, he wrote that he was not insulted, but disappointed. "I should point out that your data draws on what has already happened in the housing market. Instead, I'd ask you to consider what is *about* to happen," he wrote. That is, he was selling the future. Then, instead of making a counter offer, the seller wrote, "This doesn't mean that I do not want to negotiate. I'd just like you to consider what I've said and see if you find it convincing. In the meantime, other shoppers who are interested in my home now have a price to beat. So, thank you for helping me out with that." Now that's a gracious—and productive—response to a submarine offer.

ULTIMATELY, GET CREATIVE

It might seem strange, but the middeal deadlock is my favorite part of any negotiation. I learned at an early age how to solve a stalemate, when my childhood friend Eugene Kicklighter got into a showdown with Ricky Ricketts over a snide remark Ricky had made about Cora Mae, Eugene's youngest sister.

Everything was coming to a head one afternoon on the school bus ride home. Eugene and I sat in the second seat behind the bus driver, our usual place, and Ricky and his brothers scooted to the back row. Eugene had already asked Ricky to apologize to Cora Mae, but Ricky refused. They were deadlocked, and a fight was sure to begin as soon as we stepped off the bus on 8 Mile Post Road.

But I was sure it would be more than just Ricky and Eugene. I knew Ricky's brothers would join in, but I also knew that Eugene was big enough to defend himself and hurt others in the process—at that point, he was in the eighth grade for the eighth time, and his dad was a swamp legend for having killed a black bear with only his hands.

I knew we needed to buy some time.

As the driver, Mr. Hickox, continued on the route making his usual stops, I shuttled between Eugene at the front of the bus, and Ricky and his brothers at the back. I was trying to strike a deal to break the deadlock between Eugene's demand of an apology and Ricky's demand for a fight. At first, the negotiations were so far apart that I asked Mr. Hickox to go a slightly different route to buy some more time. He agreed to drop us all off last.

Now I had enough time to come up with an idea that would be more appealing to both sides than a fight: an arm-wrestling match at the skating rink on Saturday night. I also threw in a deal sweetener. If Eugene won, he would get his apology, and if Ricky won, he would get both of Eugene's deer tags in the upcoming hunting season.

Since Ricky already owed Cora Mae an apology, and his part of the agreement would mean only a private apology to Cora Mae, without anyone else around, Eugene wanted a little more. I was just happy to be gaining traction.

The next step in clearing the impasse was to see what each side could give at little or no cost to themselves. By swamp standards, Ricky's folks were well off; his dad owned a four-wheel drive and had a boatload of rods and reels. That gave me an idea.

"If Eugene wins, can you throw in a Zebco 33 reel—one that your dad doesn't use?" I asked Ricky. He agreed, because it didn't really cost *him* anything. Now I thought we had a deal.

Then Eugene backslid on me, saying Ricky had to *publicly* apologize because he had said the initial insult publicly. After some back-and-forth, I finally got them to agree to let Cora Mae tell everyone publicly that Ricky had apologized. That accomplished the same objective, but with slightly different means.

We were just three stops from the end of our route when Ricky demanded that he still needed more if he were the winner. This was my fault; I should have locked Ricky down when he agreed to the Zebco. Now I had to shuttle up front and ask Eugene, who was a mechanical genius, if he would repair Ricky's go-kart if Ricky won. I convinced Eugene by pointing out that, since we all drove it, he would really be fixing it for all of us.

When the bus finally rolled to a stop on 8 Mile Post Road, we had ourselves a deal. There was no fight. Instead, everyone exited satisfied that they had a win in the negotiations.

Today, when a deadlock creeps into a deal, I use many of the same tactics I used on that bus. I began by buying more time (getting Mr. Hickox to alter his route), and then used some creative dealmaking to see that everyone got something they wanted.

In the end, Eugene won the arm-wrestling match, and the only player who didn't keep to the deal was Cora Mae—she got her apology, but didn't tell a soul. Still, that was the end of the problems on that bus and it proved that deadlocks are great opportunities to push deals to higher ground.

CHAPTER NINE

THE THREE SEASONS FOR SELLING

Fast-growth entrepreneurs are often fast talkers, but one of the most valuable lessons that all entrepreneurs can learn is when to keep their mouths shut. That's especially important during exit negotiations. That's harder to do when the other person in the negotiations has learned the same lesson. The hidden rule is usually this: the one who speaks first loses.

I endured the longest negotiating pause of my life when I met with a highly successful software entrepreneur who didn't like two things: people and talking. Worse still, he had learned to play both dislikes to his advantage.

It all started when, at the entrepreneur's request, a mutual acquaintance called to introduce us. The entrepreneur had built a very profitable business around a software that served as a platform for small mortgage companies. He was ready to take a solo boat trip across the Atlantic, so he wanted to get out. "He is eccentric, a little weird—maybe a lot weird—but he is brilliant," the acquaintance told me. That should have been a sign, but I called the number the acquaintance gave me anyway.

I thought I was calling to talk to the entrepreneur. Instead, I got one of his colleagues, who seemed a little scattered and odd. She was baking a cake at work, she said, and the owner of the company had entrusted her to take care of the arrangements for me to meet with him. Just like that, there was money in my account for my trip two weeks later to visit with him where he was staying on a lake in Nevada.

When the plane landed, I picked up a rental car and drove to the lake. That's when I realized I was meeting him at a residence, not an office. The sun was setting and it was getting hard to find my way on the lake roads, but I kept going and finally found the place.

I had an uneasy feeling as I knocked on the door and then rang the bell. The place was dark, and at first, there was no response. I was actually walking away when a shirtless guy stuck his head out the door and just stared at me without a word.

Caught off guard, I sort of pointed eastward and said, "I am from Atlanta."

"OK, come in," he answered, and led me through the door. Walking through that dark house, I realized that I had no idea what game he was playing. I just knew that I was losing.

We walked through the house and out to a deck overlooking the lake. Since there was no moon, it was pitch black.

Without looking at me, he asked, "What have you done?"

I felt like things were not going in my favor, so I gave him the short version of my bio. Then, I nervously reminded him why I was there: "You asked me to come out?"

That's when he looked me straight in the eye and asked: "How much do you want?"

After having come so far, there was no way I was going to state the obvious ("Do you mean to sell your company?"). I knew that question was hanging in the air, but instead, I got straight to the point: naming a number. With just a slightly raised voice, I said, "For a company your revenue size, it will be 250 grand." I said nothing about conditions, commissions, retainers, or anything else.

Silence. He just looked at me, shook his head, then cocked one leg up on a deck rail and stared out into the lake. I followed suit, cocked one leg up on the deck rail and stared along with him. Right then I knew: If I said anything, it would be a wasted a trip.

For what seemed like an eternity, but was only ten minutes, I stood there with him, not saying a word. Finally, the agony ended. He took his foot off the rail and said, "OK, let's do it."

As I was driving back to the airport, I thought of something my grandmother said to me when I told her I was going off to college. "When you get up there," she said, "I want you to do more praying and less talking." I confess that I did not do much praying in college, but I made up for it that dark night as I walked through that house and then stood on the deck staring out at the lake.

THE WISDOM TO KNOW WHEN TO SELL

Besides knowing when to do less talking, and when to pray feverishly, an entrepreneur must understand the three seasons for selling. By now, you're familiar with the notion that there are three peaks to a company's growth cycle: hypergrowth, human scale, and financial scale (see figure 8). Knowing the benefits and hazards of *when* to exit is important to the success of your exit.

3 GROWTH PEAKS I TIME TO DECIDE

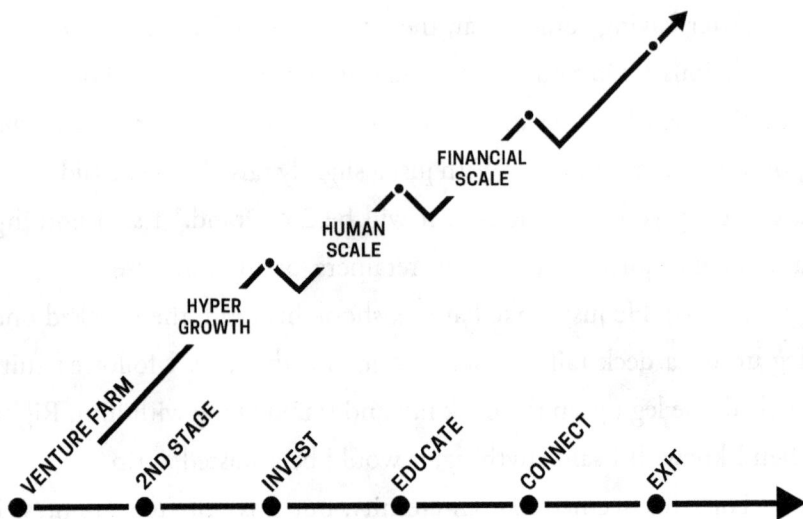

Figure 8: Time to decide.

Most entrepreneurs want to hold on to their company at the peak of a growth cycle, then sell at the bottom, when profitability is lowest. A peak is defined as the highest revenue with the lowest cost structure, until you get to the next level. But the reality is that most entrepreneurs should sell at a peak, not a trough. Why? Because after each of the three peaks, you'll need to make major infrastructure and people investments to get to the next level. If you make those investments and *then* try to sell, your company's financials will translate into a lower sale price. In other words, you could work five more years and get 50 percent less for your company! Let's keep that from happening.

Along with the asking price, *when* to sell is the most important decision you'll make. You should strategically plan to sell before making the necessary investments that follow each peak. Sell either when you hit the peak of hypergrowth, the peak of human scale, or—for the few entrepreneurs who take their companies all the way there—the peak of financial scale.

Consider how that worked for Dr. Mark McKenna, whom I mentioned in chapter 3. Originally an emerging real estate entrepreneur in New Orleans, McKenna moved to Atlanta and started a new business after Hurricane Katrina destroyed his company. McKenna sold his new company, ShapeMed, to a $2 billion publicly traded fitness juggernaut.

ShapeMed is a medical spa that grew into a low-cost wellness enterprise for the masses. McKenna's million-dollar bet was that secretaries, schoolteachers, and many other working-class professionals would want medical spa services just like their wealthier counterparts. He was correct. When ShapeMed hit the right price point, the customers came in droves. While the competition fought over 5 percent of the market, ShapeMed became the provider to *50 percent*.

But even as McKenna was engaged in the grueling work of venture farm and then hypergrowth, he found himself laughed at and shunned by his industry peers. While they paid for expensive print advertising, McKenna mastered internet promotion. His peers derided his Walmart prices and his mass-marketing techniques, so he decided to respond to their criticism in a novel way: he published his prices on billboards across the city. Even *more* customers came pouring in—and his critics were left to eat their words. "I only do the billboards to make sure my competition doesn't sleep," he told me. A good exit usually involves the creation of a new market; it gives the buyer something to own.

When McKenna hit the peak of hypergrowth, he knew it was time to sell. He was committed to following the KGE playbook, which meant that he used a gross revenue multiple, rather than EBITDA, to negotiate the price. And with ShapeMed's impressive track record, he was able to attract a great brand with a large footprint that would be able to efficiently replicate ShapeMed's business model.

This was a quintessential good exit—but it wasn't easy for a second. In addition to the usual deal-on, deal-off negotiating process that's part of any exit, a long-lost ex-employee of McKenna's (from an entirely different company) showed up and claimed that he shared company ownership. His claim wasn't based on any documents but rather on a long-ago discussion held in a restaurant.

As I told McKenna at the time, this is very common. It sometimes seems, with eight out of every ten deals, just when a lot of money appears on the table, ex-partners, ex-spouses, ex-brothers-in-law, and ex-whoevers suddenly show up and claim to own 5, 10, even 50 percent of the company. Unfortunately, if a renegade long-lost partner or relative sends an ownership claim to the buyer, the entire deal can be called off in a second, especially with big companies that don't like messy transactions. You have to take these matters head-on and, quite frankly, take some chances. When all the shouting stops, what usually sends these deal renegades packing is a good-riddance fee.

But McKenna stayed tough and stayed the course. He had doggedly grown his company and strategically chosen the right moment to sell, and he kept steering the ship until the bogus ownership claim had been dismissed. Then he made his cash exit.

LAKE LANIER, ASPEN, MONACO: HOW MUCH CASH DO YOU NEED?

There's one more important variable in the calculation of when to exit your business, and it doesn't have anything to do with the business itself.

You have to get clear on what you want.

Some entrepreneurs are obsessed with changing the world and aren't interested in anything else. For this type of person, opening a hundred locations won't be enough; they will always chase the next horizon (think Jeff Bezos).

For many other entrepreneurs, twenty stores is plenty; they've proven their idea, and they can now sell for a few million dollars. For others, opening fifty locations will be the magic number so they can exit with more than a few million dollars. I've had entrepreneurs turn down $40 million because it wasn't enough, and I've had others happily accept $5 million and plan never to work again. Based on these very different personal definitions of success, the optimal business strategy during the growth phase is different, and the timing of the exit is different too. It all depends on what you want.

That's why the KGE playbook sets solid exit standards for how much cash you'll need for the kind of life you want to live after your exit. These standards give entrepreneurs a specific goal to aim for during growth and in the exit negotiation. Remember at the end of chapter 1 when I said you should know your exit plan even before you *start* your business? This is why: when you take the time to pin down your desired future lifestyle, you can then tailor your business strategy, and your eventual exit, accordingly.

While every entrepreneur's idea of the perfect post-exit lifestyle will be different, at the Oxford Center, we took the step of creating three scenarios that roughly capture what most entrepreneurs want. These scenarios then allow you to ballpark, based on what you want and your current age, how much cash you'll need to bring in from your sale.

LAKE LANIER, GEORGIA

In this exit scenario, you purchase a four-bedroom house on a lake for $600,000 and pay off the mortgage as part of sale proceeds. Gross retirement income (pretax) is $80,000. This assumes a 25 percent combined tax rate and 15 percent capital gains rate, and no charitable contributions. (Additional assumptions listed below.)

YOUR AGE TODAY	ASSETS NEEDED AT RETIREMENT
30	$3.3 million
40	$2.6 million
50	$2.1 million
60	$1.5 million

ASPEN, COLORADO

In this scenario, you purchase two homes, once again paying off the mortgages from your sale proceeds. You buy a $1.4 million two-bedroom/two-bathroom condo in Aspen as well as a $900,000 four-bedroom home in Florida (where there is no state income tax). Gross retirement income is $500,000 a year, or $360,000 after tax. This assumes Florida residency, with a 28 percent tax rate and 20 percent capital gains rate. It also allows for 10 percent of income to be donated to a charitable legacy foundation.

YOUR AGE TODAY	ASSETS NEEDED AT RETIREMENT
30	$20 million
40	$16.5 million
50	$14.5 million
60	$12 million

MONACO (FRENCH RIVIERA)

This scenario includes several of the assumptions of the Aspen scenario: a home in Florida and a condominium in Aspen with both mortgages paid off, as well as 10 percent of income donated to a charitable legacy foundation. In addition, you purchase a $4.7 million two-bedroom apartment in the Principality of Monaco, once again paying off the mortgage. In this scenario gross retirement income is $5 million per year, or $3.35 million after tax with Florida residency, with a 33 percent tax rate and capital gains at 20 percent.

YOUR AGE TODAY	ASSETS NEEDED AT RETIREMENT
30	$172 million
40	$149 million
50	$124 million
60	$98 million

All of these scenarios assume a life expectancy of ninety years and a spouse of the same age. Scenarios assume a 5 percent average annual return on taxable monies and a 6 percent return on qualified monies such as Roth IRA accounts. All scenarios allow for 2.5 percent spending inflation year over year, assume no college costs after retirement, and assume Social Security benefits are drawn at full retirement age.

From a house on a lake to the high life in Monaco, these scenarios are intended to cover the gamut of what entrepreneurs need and want in their post-exit life. Decide which one you're shooting for—and plan accordingly.

VALUATION MODEL: DISCOUNTED CASH FLOWS

Now you have an estimate of how much money you'll need for your post-exit life. But how does that number compare to what your company is worth?

Whether you're at the peak of hypergrowth, the peak of human scale, or even the peak of financial scale, the discounted cash flows (DCF) valuation model allows you to assess the current value of your company. The DCF values a company by discounting free cash flows to a present value at the time of the valuation. In this model, the company's value is equivalent to future cash flows not leveraged by debt.

In KGE, we use the DCF valuation model because it doesn't require the information published by publicly held companies—one of the few models for which that is true. For many entrepreneurial ventures, there is no publicly held comparable, which makes it difficult or impossible to use many other models. The DCF requires no information on prior transactions or comparable companies.

This is also the best valuation method for the entrepreneur because projections of future cash flows require making some assumptions, and the entrepreneur can guide those assumptions by providing insight and projections about the future of the business.

STEPS TO CALCULATING VALUATION WITH DISCOUNTED CASH FLOWS (DCF)

1. *Calculate the discount rate.* The discount rate is used to discount future cash flows to a present-day value. The weighted average cost of capital (WACC) is the weighted average between the cost of equity and the cost of debt, also referred to as the company's cost of capital, or the rate

of return the company pays to its creditors. (This number for Oxford Center members is determined using a variety of methods, depending on the company and the industry.)

2. *Project financial statements.* The financial statements are projected as one line item at a time to show overall projections for the future of the company.

3. *Project free cash flows.* Projecting free cash flows in the DCF model takes a few steps. The first is to calculate projected EBIT (earnings before interest and taxes). Taxes are then subtracted from EBIT to get after-tax earnings. Next, depreciation is added back. After that, additions to plant, property, and equipment are subtracted. Finally, the changes in net working capital accounts are subtracted. That produces free cash flow.

4. *Determine terminal value.* The terminal value is the value of the cash flows over the life of the business. This is typically done by multiplying the fifth year's free cash flow by a terminal growth rate. A formula determines the value of all the terminal cash flows after the fifth year.

5. *Calculate present value to determine valuation.* All cash flows are divided by a yearly factor and added together to determine enterprise value. The net debt is subtracted, yielding the value of the company.

TO THE OPEN WATERS OF THE SEA

If your company is in the middle of the chaos of hypergrowth or human scale, it might be hard to imagine a day when you're done building it. And when you're in negotiations, it may be impossible to imagine the day when you're also done *selling* it.

But through the KGE playbook, I've tried to help you understand not only the exit, but the good exit. Now you have the tools to negotiate, and ultimately walk away with, every penny you can.

Once the sale has closed, you love the final price, and you have gotten what you wanted out of the business from the start, then what?

CHAPTER TEN

YOUR PATH TO THE SEA—A LIFE OF LEGACY, PURPOSE, AND FREEDOM

B y now you know this about me: I'm not a big fan of buzzwords. That's why I really don't like the fact that I'm about to use two of them. But there's no way around it, so here goes.

Once you've made your exit, it's time to start thinking about your legacy, and legacy is really about moving from *success* to *significance*.

Most entrepreneurs get into business to change the world and make a difference. They have an idea of how something can be better than the way it is now, and they set out to prove their point. They also know that, if they do it right, the money will follow.

So they create something from nothing. They start a business, and they bust their butts. For years, they think about little else besides what needs to happen next to push their business forward.

But once you've made your cash exit, you've checked all the boxes. In your corner of your industry, you *have* changed the world.

For your customers, you *have* made a difference. Once the market first began to pay attention to your solution, you were on your way to proving your point. By the time a larger company made an offer to acquire the business you started from scratch, you definitely had proven your point. And when the buyer signed, the money finally arrived.

At this point, there's no doubt about it: you're successful.

But there's one final step in KGE. Because it's not enough to be successful.

That's an audacious statement, I know. Audacious but true. It is *not* enough to be successful. How do I know? Because I know who the most miserable person in the world is.

The most miserable person in the world is a billionaire entrepreneur sitting on the beach with nothing to do.

Consider just one example. When the founder of Papa John's sold his company, he discovered something truly awful—that he just couldn't live without Papa John's. That company was his routine every day for about as long as he could remember. He went in to work, and he worked on the business. That was what he did. The business gave him structure. It was his personal mission. When that disappeared, he had no idea what to do with his days.

There is a well-known connection between attention deficit disorder (ADD), or attention deficit hyperactivity disorder (ADHD), and entrepreneurship. Some wildly successful entrepreneurs, including the founders of IKEA and JetBlue, have diagnoses of ADHD. Plenty of successful entrepreneurs think that this disorder was the key to their success, rather than a barrier they had to overcome. That makes sense when you consider that ADD and ADHD are associated with risk-taking, multitasking, inventiveness, and general high energy. Even though it's called attention "deficit" disorder, when people with this diagnosis find something they love to do, they can and do focus on it for hours on end, often to the exclusion of everything else.

For entrepreneurs, their business serves this role. And though they may appear to be all over the map, the business plays the invaluable role of keeping them structured. They *have* to go see clients, they *have* to take care of employees, they *have* to address customer complaints. There's a daily routine in that, even as every day is different. That's the structure that keeps them grounded.

And when all of that is gone, it can be very wicked. I think of this situation like a professional athlete. Athletes know they need to practice every single day. They practice today, they practice tomorrow, and then comes the day when they perform. But what happens when they can't play anymore, and all of that disappears?

This is why KGE doesn't end with the exit. You haven't come this far, and worked this hard, to be unhappy at the end of it all. The last step of KGE is your legacy—your chance to move from success to significance.

SOMETHING (ELSE) THAT REALLY LIGHTS YOUR FIRE

It just so happens that, as I put the finishing touches on this book, I'm making an exit of my own. After a decade of building the company, I recently sold the Oxford Center.

This is my second exit, and I can tell you that I didn't do a great job of managing the first one. When I sold STI in 2003, I hadn't given one moment of thought to what it would feel like to wake up the next day and have no company. It hadn't occurred to me that, over the previous eight years, a lot of my identity had become tied up in the business. After it sold, there was a while when I didn't quite know who I was.

This time around, I'm a little bit wiser. Instead of leaving the question of what's next to sneak up on me postsale, I've given a lot of thought to where I'm headed next. What I know is that it has to be something that—like my companies—really lights my fire. Whatever it is, I have to be totally passionate about it.

After I sold STI and before I founded the Oxford Center, I went to Beirut, Lebanon. There I taught at the American University of Beirut. I spent four years there, and I traveled all around the Middle East. I loved it. I loved the Lebanese culture, and I grew close with many people there. I learned that the Middle East is a hugely misunderstood region. I gained an understanding of the conflict in Palestine that I don't think I ever could have gotten by remaining on US soil.

Now that I'm making my second exit, I've thought about going back to the Middle East to help train entrepreneurs.

I've thought about how I can help bring business skills to the developing world. I've thought about going to Haiti to work with business owners there.

Broadly speaking, there are three major areas where most entrepreneurs consider leaving their legacy: philanthropy, academia, and activism. Will you give? Will you teach? Will you make a difference on an issue you care about? Maybe it's protecting wildlife. Maybe it's climate change. Only you know the answer.

What I know is that, if I were still working around the clock on my business, I wouldn't have time to be creative in other ways. I wouldn't have time to daydream. Now is that time. Maybe your own creativity and your daydreams will lead you to the place where you'll leave your legacy.

One thing I decided for sure was that I was going back to the place where I started. As I write these words, I'm planning to lead others on a trip through the muddy waters of the Okefenokee Swamp. We won't be paddling all the way through the Okefenokee to the St. Mary's River and then to the Atlantic Ocean, the way I did with my brother and cousin when I was a kid—that's for sure. I've already crossed those treacherous waters and arrived at the open waters of freedom. With your own exit behind you, so have you.

But I suppose that, no matter where I go, and what I do, I'll always feel the pull of the swamp.

ABOUT THE AUTHOR

From launching a three-time Inc. 500 Fastest-Growing Company to endowing Emory University's Executive MBA program and becoming a *New York Times* blogger on fast-growth companies, Cliff Oxford bridges the gap between Harvard and hard knocks. Oxford's talent, experience, and knowledge are highly sought after, making him the leader in entrepreneur education for emerging and growth companies.

Oxford launched STI Knowledge, which pioneered CRM technology and services. STI created a cultural phenomenon that made STI an Inc. 13 company, and earned Oxford Atlanta's Entrepreneur of the Year. STI went on to serve 86 percent of the Fortune 1000 with a global presence in Hong Kong, United Kingdom, South Africa, and more. In 2009 he created a reality television series for CBS called *The Next Tycoon*.

Under Oxford's leadership, the Oxford Center for Entrepreneurs has the vision, mission, and standards for creating entrepreneur centers that drive and escalate economic development in communities. The center combines active learning with real-world curriculum at universities and colleges.

Oxford sold Oxford Center for Entrepreneurs to the Advantage|ForbesBooks family in April 2018.

VISIT US ONLINE TO ACCESS THESE FREE RESOURCES

WHAT YOU NEED TO KNOW ONE MINUTE BEFORE DAYLIGHT

The Morning Report™ is one of the most highly anticipated daily emails for CEO entrepreneurs around the globe. In less than 2 minutes, the Morning Report provides a summary of all the essential news items that matter to people who own and run businesses.

→ **SUBSCRIBE AT <u>GETTHEMORNINGREPORT.COM</u>**

IS YOUR BUSINESS ATTRACTIVE TO A BUYER?

Thinking of selling your business? Does your company have the 7 Elements of a Valuable Business? Our 7E Assessment will uncover your core strengths, areas of weakness, and hidden assets so you can maximize the value of your most valuable asset.

→ **TAKE THE 7E ASSESSMENT AT <u>OXFORDCENTER.COM/7E</u>**
   Your score will be emailed to you within seconds of submitting

APPLY TO BE AN OXFORD CENTER MEMBER

Oxford Center for Entrepreneurs is an exclusive membership community that brings together second-stage and high-growth CEO entrepreneurs interested in accelerating their growth through education, shared insights, and commerce connections that push their thinking and businesses forward. We support our Members with our no-nonsense Know-Grow-Exit education and Entrepreneur Briefings that feature leading CEOs that have grown multimillion and billion-dollar companies.

→ **APPLY FOR MEMBERSHIP AT <u>OXFORDCENTER.COM/APPLY</u>**

www.ingramcontent.com/pod-product-compliance
Lightning Source LLC
Chambersburg PA
CBHW071844200326
41519CB00016B/4235